A must-read for any leader who cares about unity.

—John Bishop, Founding and Senior Pastor, Living Hope Church

Larry Osborne is one of my heroes, —a real "leader's leader." He has been delivering kingdom results for a couple of decades through the ministry of North Coast Church. Sticky Teams unlocks the secret of building effective leadership at every level. This is a must-read book for any leader.

—Bob Buford, Founder, Leadership Network

Larry Osborne gets the church and leadership. Finally, the "Best of Larry" is out and available for all to enjoy! These truths will shape your leadership for years to come.

—Dale Burke, Pastor and Author, First Evangelical Free of Fullerton

Addresses every aspect of organizations with commonsense, pragmatic solutions.

—Dr. Samuel R. Chand, President, Samuel R. Chand Consulting

What *Sticky Church* was to small groups, *Sticky Teams* is to church leadership. This is the most practical book I've read on the subject. *Sticky Teams* is a must-read!

—Scott Chapman, Senior Pastor, The Chapel

Captures the innovative knowledge of a proven pastor that will help you avoid the painful mistakes that will occur without proactive consideration.

—Mark DeYmaz, Directional Leader, Mosaic Church of Central Arkansas

You'll find yourself saying, "That's so true. How come I've never heard anyone say that before?" This book will help you build a team and keep them on the same page.

—Chris Dolson, Senior Pastor, Blackhawk Church

Filled with practical wisdom from one of the most insightful Christian leaders. Every leader needs to read it.

—Mark Driscoll, Pastor, Mars Hill Church

The book I needed when I landed in the jungles of my first pastorate. Destined to be a standard.

—Mark Forman, Pastor, North Coast Calvary Chapel

Addresses issues that are often avoided, from setting salaries to handling a church board to firing underperforming staff.

—Ron Forseth, General Editor, SermonCentral.com

No one has more practical, down-to-earth, but Spirit-filled wisdom than Larry Osborne.

—J. D. Greear, The Summit Church

Profound yet simple ideas that will inspire any leader to proactively implement lasting developmental changes.

—Craig Groeschel, LifeChurch.TV

Speaks to the issues pastors of growing churches face every day and offers sane and tested ways to turn those issues into fuel for the mission of Christ.

—David W. Hegg, Senior Pastor, Grace Baptist Church

Whenever someone has asked me how to handle some tricky situation around our church, I've pulled out old notes from conversations with Larry. I am stoked that I no longer have to dig up old notes. I merely have to hand out copies of *Sticky Teams*.

—Noel Heikkinen, Pastor, Riverview Church

Counterintuitive wisdom that will help you and your people flourish whether you serve a church of five, five hundred, or five thousand.

—Tom Hughes, Lead Pastor, Christian Assembly Church

In my twenty years of knowing Larry, I've described him as the guy who was asking and answering the questions the rest of us were not ready to deal with yet.

—Dr. John Jackson, Executive Director, Thriving Churches International

If you want to build a team that will impact your organization and your community, you want this book!

—John Jenkins, Senior Pastor, First Baptist Church of Glenarden

What the church needs, in every generation, is fresh perspective and seasoned experience. It's rare to find both in one voice, but that's what I've come to expect from Larry Osborne.

—James Long, Managing Editor, Outreach Magazine

Every pastor, board member, and church committee member in America ought to read and discuss this book. The chapter "What Game Are We Playing?" may have saved my ministry.

— Shawn Lovejoy, ChurchPlanters.com and Mountain Lake Church

Larry's insights are priceless on three counts: thoroughly practical, totally readable, and highly transferable to your unique leadership context.

—Will Mancini, Founder, Auxano, and Author, Church Unique

Consider this book required reading. Larry's valuable insights could save so many church leaders from serious problems.

—Mel Ming, Professor, Assemblies of God Theological Seminary

No-nonsense, in-the-trenches leadership wisdom that only Larry Osborne delivers.

—Tony Morgan, Author, Killing Cockroaches

Practical insights not just on what to do but on how to do it, and full of values that Osborne has lived out and led through over the years.

—Perry Noble, Pastor, NewSpring Church

Like a Vulcan "mind meld"—a lifetime of knowledge passed from one generation to the next. I can only imagine the land mines I could have avoided if I'd had it twenty-five years ago.

—Rick Olmstead, Pastor, Church Planter and Regional Overseer, VineyardUSA

Lots of people talk about community; few help us figure out how to build community. Larry Osborne is one of the few.

—John Ortberg, Pastor and Author, Menlo Park Presbyterian Church

This is possibly the best book on leadership ever written. Everyone should buy multiple copies.

—Carolyn Osborne, Larry's Mom

Guides leaders into some of the most important but counterintuitive keys to developing a healthy team while making room for emerging leaders. A must-read for every pastor who cares about having God-honoring, community-rich leadership for the local church.

—Darrin Patrick, Lead Pastor, The Journey

Larry Osborne is the king of common sense and counterintuitive leadership. *Sticky Teams* overflows with the insights and the wisdom of experience.

—*Scott Ridout, Sun Valley Community Church*

Full of great lessons that will help any church leader build teams that serve together better.

—*Dino Rizzo, Pastor, Healing Place Church*

Practical, sound biblical strategies to be a better leader.

—*Toby Slough, Pastor, Cross Timbers Community Church*

Whatever the size of your church, Larry has something to share on how to remove the obstacles that prevent staffs and boards from working together effectively.

—*Dr. Stacy L. Spencer, Founder/Lead Pastor, New Direction Christian Church*

One of those books you will read more than once. It is wise and practical, just like its author.

—*Ed Stetzer, President, LifeWay Research*

This is the stuff we thought they'd teach us in seminary. *Sticky Teams* is going on my list of must-read books for pastors.

—*Geoff Surratt, Author and Pastor, Seacoast Church*

If you relate to boards, lead a staff, or are thinking about starting a church, this ought to be one of the first books you purchase.

—*Greg Surratt, Lead Pastor, Seacoast Church*

A brilliant book that every ministry leader should be required to read before accepting an appointment on a board, on a staff, or as a pastor.

—*Scott Thomas, Acts 29 Director, Executive Leadership Team of Mars Hill Church*

All the young leaders I engage want Osborne as their mentor. *Sticky Teams* contains the best thinking about practical church leadership that you will find today.

—*Dave Travis, Leadership Network*

For anyone who wants a healthy functional church.

—*Ken Werlein, Founding Pastor, of Faithbridge Church*

I plan to make this book required reading for each student and intern who plans to succeed in ministry!

—*Dr. Wayne Cordeiro, New Hope Christian Fellowship*

STICKY TEAMS

Keeping Your Leadership Team and Staff *on the Same Page*

LARRY OSBORNE

ZONDERVAN®

ZONDERVAN.com/
AUTHORTRACKER
follow your favorite authors

We want to hear from you. Please send your comments about this book to us in care of zreview@zondervan.com. Thank you.

ZONDERVAN

Sticky Teams
Copyright © 2010 by Larry Osborne

This title is also available as a Zondervan ebook.
Visit www.zondervan.com/ebooks.

This title is also available in a Zondervan audio edition.
Visit www.zondervan.fm.

Requests for information should be addressed to:

Zondervan, *Grand Rapids, Michigan 49530*

Library of Congress Cataloging-in-Publication Data

Osborne, Larry W., 1952 –
    Sticky teams : keeping your leadership team and staff on the same page /
Larry Osborne.
      p. cm.
    ISBN 978-0-310-32464-5 (softcover)
    1. Group ministry. 2. Pastoral theology. 3. Christian leadership. I. Title.
BV675.O72 2010
254'.0995 – dc22
                                                   2009040181

All Scripture quotations, unless otherwise indicated, are taken from the Holy Bible, *New International Version*®, *NIV*®. Copyright © 1973, 1978, 1984 by Biblica, Inc.™ Used by permission of Zondervan. All rights reserved worldwide.

Any Internet addresses (websites, blogs, etc.) and telephone numbers printed in this book are offered as a resource. They are not intended in any way to be or imply an endorsement by Zondervan, nor does Zondervan vouch for the content of these sites and numbers for the life of this book.

Cover design: Rob Monacelli
Interior design: Melissa Elenbaas

Printed in the United States of America

---

13 14 15 16 /DCI/ 22 21 20 19 18 17 16 15 14 13

To the congregation and staff of North Coast Church

Thank you for all you've taught me
about ministry, leadership, and following Jesus.
You've been the best team and congregation
a pastor could ever hope for.

Contents

Contents

Part 3: Communication: Keeping Everyone on the Same Page

Contents

Foreword

WHEN LARRY OSBORNE TOLD me he was writing another book on ministry and leadership, I jumped at the chance to write the foreword. His first book, *The Unity Factor*, has held a dear spot in my heart ever since I read it for the first time in 2002. It was a lifesaver. I had been at Highland Village First Baptist Church (now called the Village) for about a year and was really struggling.

I'd been trained for ministry by a group of brilliant, godly men who taught me hermeneutics, Christian history, how to decline and parse Greek words, Hebrew, systematic theology, courses in Pauline literature, the Old Testament prophets, and preaching. I devoured every bit of it and learned quickly that I had a knack for theology and preaching. I spent an enormous amount of time studying the Scriptures as well as deep books written by men who had long been dead. From Luther, Calvin, Owen, Baxter, and almost any Puritan I could get my hands on, and my personal favorite, Charles Spurgeon, I learned God-honoring, Christ-exalting, Scripture-saturated doctrine from the best our great history has to offer. Every bit of it was beneficial and profitable. I needed it, and there isn't a day that passes that I'm not thankful for the tools I received.

When I graduated, I felt I had all the information I would need to accomplish all that God would demand of me as a pastor. I had a verse for everything. For the next few years, as an associate pastor over college students and as an itinerant preacher, I found very few gaps in my training and was extremely pleased with what I had paid so dearly for in money, hours, and study.

But my perception changed quickly when I became the lead pastor of the Village. It didn't take me long (about a month and a half) as a twenty-eight-year-old pastor to figure out that I had more to learn than I had time to learn. The gaps in my training weren't biblical, theological, or even philosophical. My gaps were in the areas of leadership and people.

In five years of theological training, we never talked about how to hire the right people or remove people who need to be removed. There was never a class on how to build a board or work with an existing board. There wasn't one seminar offered on how to set salaries, conduct performance reviews, or create clear job descriptions. Although the Scriptures taught me the spirit by which I was to interact with people and the grace I was to show even my enemies, I was at a loss regarding the practical aspects of leading a team — and a team of leaders at that.

After a year of making some monumental mistakes, I was venting to a good friend about how frustrated I was trying to figure these things out on my own. I felt blind and silly. He recommended a pile of books to me but told me to start with Larry Osborne's *The Unity Factor: Developing a Healthy Church Leadership Team*.

I read Larry's book in less than two days and ordered multiple copies to hand out to the deacon board and staff. Larry's insights brought a great deal of clarity for me and the men who led alongside of me. Since then, it has shaped how we view and lead our staff and the men and women God has asked us to lead.

In *Sticky Teams*, Larry builds on the kernel of his earlier writings with an additional twenty years of life lessons, wisdom, and front-line ministry experience. He clearly shows what it takes to build and maintain a unified and effective team, explains how and why growth changes everything, exposes the most common roadblocks to unity, and shares the keys to getting everyone on the same page, as well as the tools for keeping them there.

I could not recommend this book more enthusiastically, and I pray it leads to healthier ministry teams and healthier churches.

— Matt Chandler
Lead Pastor
The Village Church

Acknowledgments

TO THE ELDERS AT North Coast Church: Thank you for your incredible support over the years and for releasing me to share with the wider body of Christ the things we've learned together. From the early "dark years" to the amazing run we've had since, it's been quite a ride.

To the staff at North Coast: You're awesome. You've taught me so much about teamwork, loyalty, and commitment. Your passion, creativity, and heart for the Lord are stunning. Much of what I've learned about leadership I learned the hard way, at your expense. Thanks for not running me out of town.

A special thanks to Chris Brown: Your giftedness, support, and willingness to share the teaching load have enabled me to write the books I've written in the past few years. I would have never done it without my great confidence in your leadership, teaching, and character. It's been fun to be part of the "Two Guys from Vista" team.

To Charlie Bradshaw, Paul Savona, and Mike Yearley: It's hard to imagine what the journey would have been like without you along the way. Our conversations, challenges, victories, laughter, and tears are all part of the core fabric of God's work in my life.

To Erica Ramos and Jenna Sampson: Your insights, honesty, and careful editing have made this a far better book than it would have been without you. If the reviews are bad, it's my fault.

To Nancy: As always, I bless you for your wise advice and your kind way of delivering it. But most of all, I'm grateful that you allowed me to "marry up."

To Nathan (and Marie), Rachel, Josh (and Kara): Thanks for all the joy you bring into my life and Nancy's. My goal when you were young was that you would grow up to love God, love the church, and love that your dad was a pastor. Thanks for making it three for three. I'm a lucky man.

Finally, to my parents, Bill and Carolyn Osborne: Thanks for the love and wisdom you poured into my life. Many of the best leadership insights I ever learned were from watching how you raised Bob, Linda, and me.

Sticky Teams

What Makes Them Different?

STICKY TEAMS STICK TOGETHER. That's their defining trait. When faced with the differing agendas and clashing perspectives that every team must work through, sticky teams know how to deal with the issues at hand and still come out united in purpose and vision, with a genuine camaraderie undamaged by strong differences. In other words, sticky teams are not only productive; they're healthy.

And that's what this book is all about. Frankly, it's the team-building manual I wished I'd had when I started out. It's filled with the powerful insights and principles I've learned and shared with thousands of pastors and business leaders over the years to help them get and then keep everyone on the same page.

The foundation of this book is my earlier work, *The Unity Factor*,[1] which dealt primarily with developing a healthy board. In *Sticky Teams*, I've widened the scope to include all three of the critical relationships that a pastor must develop and maintain (with the board, the staff, and the congregation). I've also added insights and lessons I've learned from an additional twenty years of frontline ministry. One thing, however, has not changed in the least: my deep conviction that the health and long-term effectiveness of any ministry begins with the health and unity of its primary leadership teams.

Genuine Unity

One of the great beauties of a truly healthy and unified leadership team is that it experiences unity in the healthiest sense of the word. Sticky teams aren't made up of mindless clones; they're made up of widely divergent personalities and viewpoints. Their team members often disagree, but they know how to fight fair. When the battle of competing ideas is over, they march out and present a united front, setting aside their personal preferences and agendas in light of the greater good and the bigger mission.

Sadly, however, this kind of unity is hard to find. It doesn't come naturally, even in churches and organizations dedicated to serving the Prince of Peace. Too many things work against our unity.

What's Gone Wrong?

What's gone wrong? Why is unity so difficult to achieve? To begin with, there's our sin nature. It messes up everything. Add to that our differing backgrounds, biases, blind spots, and passions. We all come to the table with a different set of eyes, which often causes us to see the same things quite differently, making consensus hard to come by.

In addition, most leadership teams are saddled with traditions, policies, and organizational structures designed for a day long past. Yet as every leader knows, it's not easy to change deeply entrenched patterns and traditions, no matter how stupid they may be. In many cases, it's a rather dangerous endeavor and a foolish career move.

The result is a well-known pattern of board conflict, turf battles, staffing silos, and splintered congregations — the stuff of ministry legend and gallows humor.

But it doesn't have to be this way. It really is possible to get everyone on the same page and keep them there. A dysfunctional group can become a winning group. I know; I've done it, after getting off to a horrible start.

To create sticky teams, we must first deal with the core problem. Frankly, most books on leadership focus on creativity, vision, innovation, clarifying the mission, or aligning programs and processes. This book aims at something different. It aims to shore up the foundation of a healthy team, because even the clearest vision, greatest innovations, and most stellar programs won't make much of an eternal (or even short-term) difference if our ministry and leadership teams are mired in the deep weeds of disunity and conflicting agendas.

I have divided this book into three main sections. Each deals with a key aspect of what it takes to develop and maintain long-term organizational health and unity.

- "Landmines and Roadblocks" exposes the organizational structures, policies, and traditions that can unintentionally sabotage even the best of teams. More important, it contains strategies for avoiding these landmines and for getting around the roadblocks.
- "Equipped for Ministry" explores what it takes to *get* everyone on the same page and headed in the same direction. Specific chapters deal with board, staff, and congregational alignment.
- "Communication" examines what it takes to *keep* everyone on the same page, with a special emphasis on the dicey areas and issues of ministry — the places where communication most easily breaks down.

We'll also look at all three of the critical team-building relationships a pastor has to deal with, because if any one of these three go south, the whole ministry can go down with it. Each of these three groups needs a strategy of its own. While many principles overlap, there are also many characteristics and challenges unique to getting each group on the same page and keeping them there.

The big three are:

The Board. Whether your tradition calls them elders, deacons, directors, or simply "big shots," these are the folks who have the power to make or break your ministry. When they work well together, it's a beautiful thing. When they don't, it's everyone's worst nightmare.

The Staff. There's nothing better than a dynamic and unified staff. It's not only powerful; it's a ton of fun. But it doesn't take much to put sand in the gears. Just one staff member who is headed in a different direction, disgruntled, or quietly passive-aggressive can drain the passion and joy out of the entire team and make life miserable for whoever is stuck trying to lead the team.

The Congregation. While we won't look in great detail at what it takes to get and keep a congregation on the same page (see *Sticky Church*[2] for a more detailed look at that subject), we will explore what can be done to preempt congregational conflict and align the differing agendas that can tear apart an entire congregation.

It's my hope that these pages will enable you and your ministry team to experience the joy and productivity that comes from genuine unity. It's an incredible thing when a group of sinners saved by grace start to work together, reading from the same page, united by the same vision, reaching for the same goals, and most important, sticking together to advance the cause of the King and his kingdom rather than our own agendas and goals.

Chapter 1

The Unity Factor

The One Thing That Can't Be Left to Chance

I GREW UP IN a Christian home. My dad was a deacon. I have no idea how I ever got saved.

It's not that dad and mom were hypocritical. They were anything but. It's just that, well, Dad was a deacon. And that was enough to show me the dark side of church. It taught me early on that serving as a lay leader can be a tough assignment filled with late-night meetings, petty squabbles, acrimonious debates, and worse.

In addition, one of my best friends was the pastor's son. When the church went through a split, my family was on the other side. It was ugly, really ugly.

So I found it rather bizarre when God called me to become a pastor. I'm still not sure why I didn't pull a Jonah.

When I became the pastor of North Coast Church, the church was just three years old. I was twenty-eight. The founding pastor had recently moved on to further his schooling. But since he was a good friend of mine (he'd been an usher in my wedding) and the congregation was small, I figured it would be a rather seamless transition.

I must have been smoking something.

Six months in, I was embroiled in controversy. Attendance was steadily shrinking. Worse, the board and I were having a hard time seeing eye-to-eye on anything. I literally lay awake at night wondering what I'd do when they finally asked me to leave, or when the church split, or when a congregational meeting turned raucous.

Fortunately, none of those things happened.

Instead, with God's help, a once divided board and splintered congregation (I didn't have a staff to mess up, or that too would have been a disaster) became a tightly knit leadership team in a church now widely known for its health and unity. Along the way, I learned a ton of lessons. But none was more important than this simple truth: *A unified and healthy leadership team doesn't just happen. It has to be a priority.*

Why Worry about Unity?

I don't think it's an accident that Jesus *predicted* church growth but *prayed* for unity. If left unattended or taken for granted, unity quickly disappears. Unity is the one thing that can't be left to chance. You'd think I would have known that based on my early church experiences. But I didn't.

That's because I chalked up conflict to sin, and of course when I quarreled with somebody, most of the sin was on "their" part. I had no idea that organizational disunity was more the norm than the exception. I had no clue that personality differences, differing perspectives, and even organizational structures could cause good people to do bad things.

I should have.

From Aaron and Miriam's harsh criticism of Moses, to Paul and Barnabas's heated argument and eventual split over John Mark, to Euodia and Syntyche's sharp clash at Philippi, to last week's big mess at First Church, God's people and God's leaders have had a hard time getting along. It's nothing new.

But I thought we would be different. I assumed that as long as we put good people on the team and stayed focused on the Lord and the Great Commission, harmony would naturally follow. If you would have told me to slow down and focus on camaraderie and unity, I would have chided you for your self-centered, holy-huddle approach to ministry. We had a world to conquer and disciples to make.

I was wrong. I didn't realize the power organizational problems have to create and exasperate spiritual problems.

As things steadily got worse, it finally dawned on me that we were never going to change the world *out there* if we couldn't solve the conflicts *in here*. So I did something I never thought I'd do. I set aside all of my ministry and church-growth goals and, for the next two and a half years, focused on molding a cohesive leadership team. I made it my number one priority.

It was a move made out of desperation, but it was one of the best moves I ever made. It changed everything. So much so that to this day I consider maintaining the unity of our board and our staff as one of my most important leadership priorities, far ahead of other worthy goals — including even evangelism, church growth, and community outreach — because without unity, everything else falls apart.

But unity doesn't just happen. You have to work at it day after day, because if you don't, it quickly slips away. And once it does, it won't matter how clear your vision is or how gifted your team is. When the foundation rots, it's not long until the whole house collapses.

It All Starts with the Board

When it comes to building a healthy and unified ministry team, it all starts with the board. As the board goes, so goes the rest of the church.

Mark my words. If the board room is a war zone, it doesn't matter what kind of revival you're having in the sanctuary. If the infighting continues, it won't be long until there's a coup d'état or a resignation. I guarantee it.

That's what happened to my friend Brian. When he took over a struggling church, he assumed that the unanimous call of the board meant that everyone was ready to move on to the next level. He came armed with vision, ideas, and a game plan to get there.

What he didn't take into account was the close friendship that two of his board members maintained with the previous pastor. When

Brian began to make changes, they took each one as a personal affront to his predecessor. They began to resist nearly everything he proposed.

From the congregation's viewpoint, things were great. After years of decline, attendance and giving were way up. Young families poured in. Evangelism and community impact were at an all-time high.

But that's not the way the board saw it. Poisoned by the continual complaints of the two ringleaders, they catastrophized every complaint and criticism they heard from an unhappy parishioner. The difference between their perspective and the congregation's was amazing. The board thought the church was on the edge of disaster. The congregation thought it was on the edge of revival.

But no matter how much affirmation Brian received from the congregation, no matter how many people came to Christ, no matter how fast the church grew, it was still the board to whom he reported. They set his salary, approved or vetoed his ideas, and controlled much of what he could and could not do.

After five years of frustration and constant battling, Brian finally quit. He and his wife decided life was too short to spend it skirmishing with the very people who were supposed to have his back. The congregation never saw it coming. They were in total shock. Before it was over, the church was decimated, a mere shell of what it had been under his ministry.

Sadly, Brian's story is not unique. It's all too common. I've heard it time after time. My guess is that you have too. But I've seldom, if ever, heard the opposite: a riled up congregation driving out a pastor who has a supportive and unified board.

That's because as the board goes, so goes the rest of the church. And that's why I always recommend focusing on unifying your board, even before the staff and the congregation. Your board needs to be healthy, unified, and working together, because otherwise, everything else soon goes south.

The Unseen Realm

There's another reason why unity, not only within the board but also among the staff and congregation, needs to be a priority.

It's the impact that sinful bickering and division have in the unseen realm.

Think of what happened when Achan pilfered some of God's spoils from Jericho. It probably seemed like a small thing to Achan. But it sabotaged Joshua's battle plan at Ai. Innocent people died, not because Joshua's battle plan was inadequate but because one man's sin had created a major spiritual disruption in the unseen realm. And that disruption had disastrous consequences.

I don't know all the details about how the unseen realm works. I'll leave that to others. But I've been in ministry long enough to know that what goes on behind the scenes and in the hearts of God's people has a huge impact on what goes on in our churches.

It's been my experience that whenever a board or staff suffers from significant conflict (whether it's a civil war or a cold war), the whole congregation suffers — even when the conflict is largely kept under wraps. Sin has a way of leaking out.

And make no mistake. Festering conflict and disunity are sin. Jesus said some strong things about forgiveness, bearing with one another, and love. When the church board, staff members, or simply a group of folks in the congregation refuse to heed his words, we can hardly expect God to bless us with spiritual power and fruit.

That's why maintaining unity is so important. It not only impacts organizational health; it impacts spiritual health and power.

○

As a pastor, it's my job to help people move along to spiritual maturity, to make sure that as a church we're fulfilling both halves of the Great Commission: leading people to Christ and nurturing them on to full obedience.

I used to think that could be accomplished by putting together challenging sermons, forming great small groups, and helping people to identify and use their spiritual gifts. I still consider these things to be important. But I now realize that I was leaving out a vital first step: creating an environment conducive to spiritual growth, which means removing the divisions, turf battles, and bitterness that sabotage the work of the Spirit.

As a farmer needs to clear the land before planting his crop, a pastor needs to clear out any conflict within the board, staff, or congregation in order to plant and reap a spiritual harvest.

And if you can't weed out all the conflict, get rid of what you can. It will make a huge difference.

Defining Unity

So what does unity look like in a church board or ministry staff? How can we know what we're aiming for?

Unfortunately, unity can be hard to define. It's a vague term. While we easily recognize its presence or absence, few of us have taken the time to carefully spell out its essential elements. Yet defining exactly what we're looking for is an all-important first step if we're serious about developing and maintaining a unified leadership team on any level.

When I first decided to make unity a priority, I realized that I had no way to measure it. When I started asking practical questions about what it looked like, the answers weren't as clear as I'd expected.

Did unity allow room for doctrinal disagreement? If so, how much was too much? Could we have a split vote and still be unified, or did unity mean unanimity? How close were our relationships supposed to be? Did unity mean being best buds? Did we have to share Thanksgiving dinner?

Eventually, I settled on three irreducible minimums that defined what I was looking for. They became the grid through which I judged how we were doing and what we were aiming for on both a board and a staff level. They form my working definition of a unified leadership team. Your list may differ. But this is a good place to start.

1. Doctrinal unity
2. Respect and friendship
3. Philosophical unity

Doctrinal Unity

I've found that the first component of a unified and healthy leadership team is doctrinal unity. By doctrinal unity, I mean agreement with our church's statement of faith, not necessarily total theological or political uniformity.

Every church has an irreducible theological minimum. For some, it's a lengthy and detailed document. For others, it's a few brief statements. Either way, for the sake of integrity, it's important that those in leadership honestly adhere to it.

But after that, we're wide open. If Jesus put Simon the Zealot (an insurrectionist who hated the Roman occupiers) on the same team as Matthew the tax collector (a collaborator with the Romans) and then made them room together, I'm not sure why we can't have some strong differences on the hot-button issues of our day and still march together under the banner of unity.

In fact, unity that insists on uniformity isn't unity at all. It's a cheap counterfeit. Genuine and biblical unity is found in the midst of real and passionate differences that we set aside in the recognition that the differences we have are nowhere as important as the King we serve.

Let's admit it. Our Christian hot buttons constantly change. One decade's battleground is another decade's yawn. At North Coast Church, we once had to navigate the passionate differences between charismatics and cessationists, pre-tribbers and post-tribbers, those who enjoyed a glass of wine and those who saw any use of alcohol as a dangerous sellout. Today the battles tend to be found in other realms: politics, the environment, or the finer points of theology. No doubt you and your church have your own hot buttons that flow out of the unique cultural setting, background, and theological pedigree of your ministry.

So how can we allow for this kind of diversity without blowing everything up? The key is to clearly determine ahead of time the things we *won't* fight about and then make it crystal clear to everyone that these issues are off-limits.

For instance, at North Coast everyone in leadership understands that we're on the welcoming committee, not the programming committee, when it comes to the Lord's return. They know that we're apolitical as an organization. We don't take public stands on candidates or propositions. They know we're all about obedience and a high view of Scripture, but arguments over limited atonement or God's offer of salvation to all are off-limits. And the list goes on.

That doesn't mean that our board members and staff aren't free to have strong opinions. It simply means they can't try to force everyone into their mold. It's okay if they see something as an important issue, even a very important issue. It's not okay if they treat it as the most important issue, one to divide and fight over.

Making clear what you will and won't fight over will save you lots of grief. In nearly every theological tussle I've been asked to moderate, the battle hasn't been over something spelled out in the church's doctrinal statement. It's been over a peripheral issue that someone felt should have been an essential issue.

If we don't spell out ahead of time what we won't fight over, sooner or later someone will add their favorite doctrine or political issue to the list of essentials and then wage war on all those who disagree.

Respect and Friendship

The second component of a unified and healthy ministry team is respect and friendship. That doesn't mean everyone has to be best friends. But it does mean that we must get along well enough to avoid the miscommunication, stereotyping, and personality conflicts that so easily get in the way when it's time to tackle a tough or difficult issue.

Yet I've found that many boards (and even some staffs) are filled with strangers. They may know one another's name and have a casual acquaintance, but that's about it.

When I arrived at North Coast Church, one board member was going through serious psychological difficulties, and another's marriage was on the rocks. Yet none of the rest of us had a clue. With those kinds of superficial relationships, it's no wonder we found unity hard to come by.

Concentrating on developing camaraderie paid rich dividends. It made serving on the board an enjoyable experience. Instead of having a hard time getting people to serve, we suddenly had a hard time getting anyone to leave.

It also radically changed the dynamic of our meetings. Friends and strangers have very different patterns of relating to one another. Friends are vulnerable, while strangers hold their cards close to the vest; friends tend to give each other the benefit of the doubt, while strangers are cautious and suspicious; and when it comes to dicey issues, friends debate, while strangers argue.

Philosophical Unity

The third component of a healthy and unified team is philosophical unity. Simply put, this means having a basic agreement about our priorities and methods of ministry.

Philosophical unity is harder to develop than doctrinal unity or sincere friendships because it can take a long time to hammer out a consensus. In our case, it was nearly four years before I could honestly say we were all headed in the same direction and in agreement as to the best path to get there.

But once we were in agreement, everything became easier. We no longer had to go back to square one on every issue or with every new board member or staff hire. We'd already established our basic direction and how we would get there.

Just as with doctrinal unity, philosophical unity doesn't mean everyone has to think alike. It's not a casting call for clones or even unanimity; there's plenty of room for disagreement. But if we're going to work together effectively, we have to be reading off the same sheet of music. Otherwise, we'll be like a small ensemble to which everyone brings his own favorite arrangement. The resulting sounds will be chaos, not music.

If you think about it, most church fights aren't over theology or even ministry goals; they're over priorities and methodology. When Dave and Pat argue over how to spend money (whether to set it aside for a new building or use it to hire a youth pastor), they're arguing over priorities. When Kelly and Walt debate the merits of a choir versus guitars and big subwoofers, they're arguing over methods. Both want to worship the Lord; they just disagree on the best way to go about it.

That's why developing and nourishing a shared philosophy of ministry is one of the most important things a pastor, board, and staff can do to maintain unity.

○

Making unity a top priority has paid huge dividends. A few years after deciding that it was something I couldn't leave to chance, I asked a new member who had been involved in many churches over the years why she and her husband had settled at North Coast.

"There were two reasons," she said. "First, we couldn't believe the lack of pressure to join. And second, we've never been in such a unified church. Usually, after you've been around for a while, when you get together in smaller groups, you hear people complaining about the board, the pastor, or the staff. We've never heard that. Maybe we don't hang around with the right people!"

On the one hand, her answer made my day. It told me how far we'd come. But on the other hand, I found it discouraging, a reminder that in more churches than I'd like to think, unity remains the missing ingredient.

Perhaps that's why the apostle Paul penned these words in his letter to the Ephesians: "Make every effort to keep the unity of the Spirit through the bond of peace."[3]

Apparently, he too believed that unity is one of those things that shouldn't be left to chance.

Part 1

LANDMINES AND ROADBLOCKS

_____

The Traditions, Policies, and Structures
That Unintentionally Sabotage Unity

_____

The dysfunction and disunity in our churches often is not so much
a matter of sinful people with evil motives as it is a pattern of failed
traditions, policies, and structures that unintentionally tear us apart.

There is a better way.

Chapter 2

Why Boards Go Bad

Structured for Conflict

WHAT IS IT ABOUT board meetings that brings out the worst in us?

For the most part, church boards are made up of good and godly people. They sincerely want to serve God. But something strange seems to happen the moment the meeting starts.

A normally good-natured parishioner suddenly morphs into an ardent lobbyist or a hypersuspicious watchdog. Folks who never balance their checkbook at home feel compelled to review and critique every dime in the budget. And business leaders who easily blow off criticism in the workplace panic over the slightest negative comment overheard in the hallway.

How did it get this way? Why do so many boards go bad?

The culprit is not what you may think. In the midst of dysfunction and chaos, we instinctively tend to chalk it up to sin and carnality. But more often than not, it's not sin that wreaks havoc; it's our systems, policies, and traditions. In many cases, we've unwittingly structured ourselves for conflict and division.

My First Board Meeting

I'll never forget my first board meeting at North Coast Church. The meeting began with prayer and devotions. But while Jim tried hard to minister to our hearts, hardly anyone listened. A couple of guys leafed through the financial statements. One doodled. Others stared off into space.

Then after a brief round of reports, we moved on to the business at hand. I assumed we were in for a short meeting. The only action item was the purchase of tires for a church-owned car. The previous pastor had used it, but since I had no need or desire to use it, I hadn't even given it a thought.

I should have.

It sparked a full-scale debate. Two members squared off over the relative merits of new tires versus retreads. They went at it for what seemed like an hour. Finally we voted. The new tires won in a split decision.

And this was for a car no one wanted and no one used.

That night on the way home, I remember thinking, "So this is what my dad went through all those years. No wonder he couldn't wait for his term to end."

Frankly, I was in a bit of shock. Since all of my previous ministry experience had been as a youth and college pastor, I had never actually been in an elder, deacon, or board meeting. I had no idea what I had been missing, or how grateful I should have been for being shut out.

The thought of going through this drill once a month for the rest of my ministry career was depressing. But it got worse. In the next few months the debates switched from what kind of tires to buy to which of my new ideas should be shot down first.

Now that was really depressing.

Five Major Roadblocks to Unity

As I agonized over what was happening, it became obvious to me that many of the problems we faced were more organizational than spiritual. It wasn't sin and pride as much as our systems and traditions that were tearing us apart.

That sent me on a mission to identify and remove every systemic and structural roadblock to our unity and effectiveness that I could find. By the time I finished (and we were unified), it was clear that out of all the dumb things that we had been doing, five things had created the most conflict. Resolving these five issues provided the biggest payoffs once we found a way to get around them or fix them.

1. Meeting in the wrong place
2. Ignoring relationships
3. Not meeting often enough
4. Constant turnover
5. Too many members

Meeting in the Wrong Place

One of the most common and frequently overlooked roadblocks to unity is location. Too many church boards meet in rooms that are cramped, uncomfortable, and poorly lit — or oversized, cold, and sterile. We often ignore the fact that environment has a huge impact on the way we behave and interact with one another.

I once met with a board that sat in rigid rows, with most members staring at the back of one another's head. It's no wonder they never had a quality discussion.

I've met with boards seated around folding tables in the middle of a large, garishly lit Sunday school room. The cold and stiff way these boards went about their business was a perfect match for the cold and sterile environment they met in.

At the other extreme, I've met with boards in exquisite, wood-paneled conference rooms. While the cushy chairs and beautiful tables provided a nice touch, the sight lines were terrible. Worse, whenever a difficult issue or strong disagreement arose, people seemed to respond in ways far more appropriate to a corporate setting than a ministry setting.

Location and environment matters; it's never neutral. It always works for us or against us. More important, it sends a strong message about what kind of behavior is expected and appropriate.

That was certainly the case when I first came to North Coast. We had no facility to call our own, so we held our monthly board meetings in my office, a refurbished two-car garage. There, on the first Thursday of every month, I witnessed a mysterious transformation. What had earlier in the day been a place of study and prayer turned into a battleground of ideas and personalities. Members who had been warm and friendly on Sunday turned critical and petty on Thursday night. Folks who took copious notes of everything I said in the pulpit now questioned everything I said in the board meeting.

Then one day, after a particularly rough meeting, I suggested we hold our next board meeting at my home. I figured the change in ambience couldn't hurt, and it might help.

Bingo.

Everything changed, so much so that from that point on, we've always met in homes.

By changing the environment, I had inadvertently changed behavioral expectations. Right away I noticed that we were noticeably more cordial when dealing with dicey issues. When reviewing the budget, we weren't quite so picky. When someone talked, no one rudely leafed through reports, even if they wanted to. Instead, they followed the unwritten rules of our society. When someone talks to you in the living room, you're supposed to listen. And when you disagree — no matter how much you disagree — when you're sitting on my couch, you're not allowed to be a butthead about it.

Admittedly, there are a few times when a large conference table or more formal setting might be better — for example, when hammering out budget details or anything else highly detailed. But in most cases, the more informal and intimate environment of a home works marvelously when it comes to building and maintaining a healthy and unified team.

Now, I realize that not every board has the luxury of meeting in a home. Some boards are too large, and some may not have an adequate home available. But nearly every board can find ways to significantly increase the warmth and informality of its meeting place. Just do what you can. You'll notice an immediate difference.

Ignoring Relationships

A second roadblock we had to overcome was our tendency to put business concerns far above relational concerns. Like many lay leaders, most of our board members defined their role in terms of their task. They saw their job as making decisions and setting direction. Anything else was a waste of time or a distraction.

I remember opening one meeting with a series of get-acquainted questions. The next morning over breakfast, our chairman informed me that elder meetings were not the proper time for such nonsense. "We have too much work to do," he said. "We have plenty of other times and places for socializing."

His mindset — that meetings exist for business and business only — is one of the main reasons why board members and staff members alike tend to view prayer and devotions as the preliminaries to the "real meeting" and why few agendas ever include time for cultivating relationships.

As I began to look for ways to emphasize relationships without making it feel like an encounter group, the first step was to schedule an all-day retreat. We jammed into a van and headed south for an old resort hotel. As we traveled and ate together, we shared many experiences. We smiled as a die-hard union man and a top-level executive exchanged barbs. We listened intently as one member explained the pressures he had been feeling at work. For most of us, it was the first time we had any idea he was considering a move. By the time we arrived home, we had experienced more laughter, kidding, and deep personal dialogue than in all our previous meetings combined.

While retreats are powerful, there are many other ways to emphasize relationships. You don't have to get away overnight. Some boards eat together before each meeting. Others regularly schedule social events. A simple way to increase social interaction among board members is to schedule a refreshment break in the middle of your meetings. This forces everyone, even those who tend to arrive late and leave early, to spend some time socializing. A little small talk goes a long way when it comes to breaking down walls.

Paying attention to relationships pays big dividends. It soothes feathers and calms the waters when disagreements and difficult issues have to be tackled. It paves the way for better business decisions, because as we've already seen, whereas strangers fight and argue, friends discuss and debate.

Not Meeting Often Enough

Another roadblock to unity is the tendency that most boards have to meet as infrequently as possible. The last thing most of us want is another meeting. Our board was no exception.

Each summer, when vacations made it difficult for everyone to get together, we ended up skipping a meeting. Add another emergency or a scheduling conflict, and it wasn't unusual for us to meet as few as ten times a year. While this may have been great for freeing up busy schedules, it messed with our board's unity.

A corporate executive, self-employed contractor, middle manager, and school administrator will always see things differently. Their educational and professional backgrounds give them radically different points of reference. The man who argued for putting retreads on the church car was a longtime hourly wage earner. He and his wife loved garage sales. The person who insisted on new tires had a management background and had never bought anything secondhand in his life.

Getting such diverse people on the same page requires getting them to spend time together. So I did something I never thought I would do: I scheduled an extra monthly meeting.

We called this extra meeting a "shepherding meeting." I'll discuss it in more detail in chapter 10, but for now, it's important to note that no votes or business decisions were allowed. This meeting wasn't for lobbying. It was for relationships. We focused on prayer, team building, instruction in practical ministry, and seeking a common vision.

I started this monthly meeting to take advantage of an important principle of group dynamics: "Whenever a group of people increase the amount of time they spend together, there is a corresponding increase in their regard and appreciation for one another."[4]

While admittedly there are some individuals we appreciate less the more time we spend with them, the dynamic of a group is different. Groups predictably draw closer with increased interaction and time.

These "shepherding meetings" paid incredible dividends. They allowed us to develop a much broader backlog of shared experiences and information, not only about the issues we talked about but also about each other and the differing backgrounds and perspectives we each brought to the table.

The fact is, many of the fiercest conflicts and battles in a church board are triggered by differing experiences and paradigms that we aren't even aware of. We can be using the same words but completely different dictionaries. Without adequate time spent together, it's hard to accurately understand and appreciate these differences, and it's much more likely that conflict will break out.

Spending extra time together is especially important for a larger board. The more people we have, the less likely it is that any one board member will have one-on-one interaction with all the other members. Large boards always have a higher "stranger" quotient.

Yet ironically, the larger a board gets, the more likely it is to schedule fewer (and longer) meetings in the hope of enabling everyone to attend. While this may cut down on absenteeism, it also sabotages cohesiveness and unity.

Constant Turnover

Another significant roadblock to our unity and health as a leadership team was the constant turnover legislated by our church's constitution.

As with many churches, our board members served three-year terms, with the terms staggered. That meant that each year, one-third of our board members rotated off the board to be replaced by a new group of elders.

On the surface, this approach appeared to have some significant advantages. It guaranteed a mix of new blood and experience. It cut down on recruitment, since only one-third of the board had to be replaced each year. It assured continuity, since two-thirds of the board always had at least a year's experience. It also made it difficult for a clique to monopolize power. And the greatest advantage may have been that it offered a gracious way to remove an ineffective or divisive board member. Just wait three years, and that person would be gone.

Despite these apparent benefits, our rotating board did more harm than good. Imagine a corporation that changed one-third of its leaders every ten to fifteen meetings. The lack of continuity would give rise to constant jockeying for position. Little work would get done. Then, just about the time the group started to gel, it would be time for another changing of the guard. No one would dream of running a company like that. But that is exactly how we were running our church.

Our high rate of turnover made developing and maintaining a cohesive team extremely difficult. When, by definition, thirty-three percent of the board lacked a corporate memory, it was hard to build on past decisions. Old battles were refought year after year. Faced with complex decisions, new members wanted to go back to square one, unable or unwilling to build on past decisions and discussions in which they had no part. It was a disaster.

While I believe some turnover is good and even necessary, in most cases, one-third is way too much. To solve this, some boards allow people to serve two terms in succession before asking them to take a sabbatical. That takes care of the high, thirty-three percent annual turnover rate and can provide a painless way to remove painful people. But let's not forget that it also forces out the good ones as well. Once a term is up, there is no way to keep a person on the board, even if that person is desperately needed.

I remember working with one church that had its two best lay leaders rotate off the board soon after losing their senior pastor. The church desperately needed their leadership and wisdom. But they were shut out of the system, unable to use their God-given gifts and wisdom, until they had waited out a forced sabbatical that no one wanted.

Frankly, there are other ways to remove painful people from the board. Perhaps the best way is to keep them off the board in the first place (which we will discuss in the next chapter). But assume that the damage has been done and a toxic member already has a position on the board. At the risk of sounding simplistic, I've found the best solution to be prayer and honest confrontation. Neither is painless or easy, but both are rather biblical.

To solve the problem of constant turnover, we changed to a system in which board members are elected to one-year terms that can be renewed indefinitely. That removed the lack of accountability that comes with a lifetime appointment, while ensuring that we could keep our best board members for as long as needed.

We have some board members who've served over twenty years. They've not grown stagnant; they've grown wise. And as long as they aren't trying to live in the past or remake us into the church we were twenty years ago, their years of continuity and corporate memory provide the rest of the team with a great gift.

To ensure that our board members don't become out of touch with (or unaccountable to) the congregation, each elder is subject to an annual reelection — not as a slate, but as individuals. We use a simple yes/no ballot, and we ask everyone who votes no to write the reason for their vote next to the person's name. So far, we've never had a candidate rejected by the congregation, and I expect we never will, because our candidates are carefully screened. But we take every no vote seriously and review it with the board member involved.

This system has given us the best of both worlds. We aren't forced to lose our best elders at an inopportune time. But the natural ebb and flow of life (shifting work schedules, relocation, and other life-change issues) guarantees that fresh blood won't be shut out. It also allows us to determine each year whether we need more or fewer elders. And most important, it eliminates one of the most common roadblocks to unity and effective teamwork: constant turnover.

Too Many Members

Size is another structural roadblock to unity. When a board, ministry staff, or executive team gets too big, it's hard to get anything done. Last week I talked to a pastor who has twenty-five members on his board. It's no wonder they move at the speed of an arthritic snail.

The larger the size of a board, the greater the temptation for board members to think of themselves as representing a particular constituency. If there are seven of us, I feel compelled to care for the whole organization. If there are twenty of us, I'm much more likely to watch out for my own.

Large boards also have a harder time communicating. The larger the group, the more likely it is that only extroverts and the strong-willed will speak out. That sets the stage for lots of after-the-meeting meetings, where those who disagreed but were afraid to speak up finally speak their mind, providing a hotbed for festering grievances and the passive-aggressive resistance of those who felt powerless in the bigger meeting.

Larger groups also tend to kill off change and innovation. Their natural discomfort with conflict and desire for harmony causes them to quickly table or shut down any new idea that someone strongly objects to. Rather than working through issues, they run from them. The result is that in any large group, the most powerful members tend to be the people who are most stubborn and angry. All they have to do is raise their voice, turn beet red, or dig in their heels, and the rest of the group will usually cave in.

I don't think this is what Paul had in mind when he went around appointing elders. These are hardly the kind of people most of us want running the church. But they're exactly who has the most power and sway in many ministry teams (and church staffs), especially once the team grows too large.

At North Coast, I've found twelve members to be the absolute maximum we can handle on our board and still have full, honest, and vulnerable conversations. Each time we've grown larger, conflict and miscommunication quickly increased. And each time we did so, it wasn't long until we fell into the family-systems trap; that's when everyone takes on a role and sticks to it. It's a trap you know you've fallen into when you don't need to go to the meetings anymore because you already know ahead of time exactly what will happen — who will say what and when they will say it.

It's boredom personified.

To keep our board small enough for full and honest debate but large enough to provide the differing perspectives, we try to keep it between seven and eleven members. As I write this, we have eleven on our board, counting me and three staff elders. At this size, the board's introverts and extroverts both engage. The stubborn and angry have a much harder time taking control. More important, by staying right-sized, we've been able to lead a massive church just as easily, wisely, and healthily as we led the smaller church we used to be.

One story sums up the difference that removing these five structural roadblocks made to the unity and health of our ministry and team.

A board member came to my office to tell me that due to a change in work schedule and other commitments, it would be impossible for him to continue to serve another year.

As we talked, his eyes filled with tears. I knew him well, but I had never seen him cry before. He wasn't the type. For a while he said nothing. When he finally spoke, he said simply, "I'm going to miss everyone, I really am."

Though disappointed to lose his service, I couldn't help myself; as soon as he left my office, I let out a shout, leaned back in my chair, and sat there with a silly grin.

It hadn't been that long ago when board members looked forward to the day their term would be over. We had finally turned the corner. Someone had cried over leaving.

We'd come a long way from arguing over new tires or retreads.

Chapter 3

Guarding the Gate

No Guts, No Unity

IT'S HARD TO HAVE a winning team with losing players, which is why guarding the gate is one of the most important tasks of leadership.

Think what happens when just one contentious or negative person joins the team. People start to walk on eggshells. Meetings become an exercise in conflict avoidance, and important initiatives are sidetracked or tabled in the hope that later discussion will somehow miraculously forge an agreement. Laughter and joy all but disappear. Off-the-record discussions and after-the-meeting meetings conspire to sabotage or change everything you thought you'd decided the night before. In short, it's a real drag.

The same thing happens when an unproductive or toxic staff member comes aboard. Those who can't cut it doom their area of ministry (and eventually the entire ministry) to mediocrity, while those who don't fit in or refuse to play well with others (even if their area of ministry is a smashing success) quickly kill morale.

But worst of all, once a toxic board member or a troublesome staff member has a seat on the bus, it can take an act of God to get them off. Removal can be an incredibly difficult process.

That's because even the most disruptive board member and unproductive staff members have friends and supporters. Getting them off the bus usually results in their friends and supporters leaving the church as well, and they seldom go quietly.

I'm sure that's why most of us choose to wait out a troublesome board member rather than face the issue head-on and why most of us do nothing about failing staff members except complain and pray that an unsuspecting church will hire them away.

Unfortunately, that's not a prayer God is likely to answer — unless, of course, he's really ticked off at the other ministry.

The best time to remove a problem player is *before* they have a place on the team. Yet if we're not careful, guarding the gate can look like a power grab. It can leave a pastor open to accusations of becoming a dictator or modern-day Diotrephes.[5]

So here are some things to keep in mind. Most of these principles apply equally to the selection of both board and staff members. But let's start by looking at a few that apply specifically to guarding the gate to the boardroom. Then we'll look at those that apply to selecting both board and staff members before ending with a few that apply especially to hiring and building a winning staff team.

Find a Way to Be Part of the Process

When it comes to selecting staff members, most pastors have lots of say. But when it comes to selecting board members, many of us have been told that it's not our place to guard the gate. We're shut out of the process by polity or tradition.

That was the case when I first came to North Coast. The tradition in my denomination (not the official polity, just the way we'd always done things) locked me out of the room. But having already experienced the painful results of silence, I decided I'd rather die on the hill of seeking a place in the selection process than die the slow, agonizing death of organizational cancer.

Make no mistake: someone is already guarding the gate. The only question is, Are these the people we want standing guard?

I was in one church when an announcement was made asking anyone who wanted to serve on the nominating committee to show up the next Tuesday night in the fellowship hall. If you came, you served. I've been in other churches that allow any member who shows up at an all-church business meeting to make a nomination from the floor. Still others seek a carefully chosen cross section of the congregation — a stay-at-home mom, a career woman, a businessman, a senior citizen, and a young adult — as if demographics are the key to wisdom.

Selecting leaders is too important to be treated this casually. It demands the best people we've got. In fact, your nominating committee (whether it's an official committee or ad hoc group) may be the most important committee in your church. It serves like the headwaters of a river. When there's pollution upstream, it eventually defiles everything downstream.

That's why I believe the pastor should always take part in the process. Even if tradition or denominational polity doesn't allow an official role, there's always an unofficial or informal way to have influence. The wise pastor will find it and take it, and the wise board will find a way to make it happen.

Intentionally keeping the pastor out of the selection process (or worse, putting someone on the board who is at personal or philosophical odds with the pastor) is like saddling a coach with a general manager and assistant coaches who don't buy into his game plan. It simply doesn't work. All it does is guarantee a series of short-term pastorates.

Speak Up or Shut Up

Yet the opportunity to speak up doesn't do much good if we lack the courage to do so.

One day while complaining about a particular feisty board member, a friend asked me how this person ever got on the board in the first place. I told him that the congregation had elected him and that I'd seen the problem coming the moment he'd been nominated.

Then my friend asked me a tough question. "Why didn't you say something beforehand?"

I told him, "It's not my place. Besides, if word ever got out, he and his friends would have my head."

Then my friend said something I didn't want to hear. It was painful, but true. "If you don't have the guts to speak up on the front end, you don't have the right to complain on the back end. So shut up — and speak up next time."

Ouch.

But he was right. I took his advice to heart. I decided that the next time we nominated elders, I would speak up about my relational concerns as readily as I spoke up about moral and doctrinal concerns.

I still remember the first time I did so. The name of a good and godly former elder had been put forward. His character and integrity were beyond reproach. But everyone in the room knew that he and I had some issues. He had approached his previous term on the board as a self-appointed watchdog, with the particular mission of making sure that I didn't get away with anything or gain too much power. Numerous times we'd sparred over silly issues.

When our nominating committee came to his name, there was an uncomfortable silence. Everyone knew there would be problems. They would be philosophical, not spiritual, but problems nonetheless. After what seemed like an eternity, I swallowed hard and spoke up, "I don't think we should have him run; if he's elected, we'll end up spending all our meetings going around in circles."

As soon as I spoke up, a couple of others spoke up in agreement. My candor had broken the ice. Apparently, they felt as strongly as I did, but they assumed that no one else noticed or that it was politically incorrect to say so. After a brief discussion, we came to a unanimous decision to nominate someone else.

Obviously, my decision to get involved in the process carried some risks. There is always the chance that something I say will get back to the person I've sidelined. But that's a risk that I'll live with. Our nominating team is made up of top-quality people. They don't have a problem remembering that "what is said here should remain here." And in case anyone is prone to forget, I remind them regularly!

But I'll also admit that secrets are hard to keep, and a pastoral veto has the potential for creating great hurt. So I'm always careful with what I say and how I say it. I hope the things I say won't be repeated. But just in case they are, I word them in such a way that I can live with it.

Look for Leaders, Not Representatives

I've also learned that it's important that our board and staff members think of themselves as leaders, not representatives.

Many churches opt for a representative model. It fits well with our American democratic principles. It aligns with the priesthood of all believers. It ensures that everyone has a chance to be heard, not just those who are powerful or well connected. It helps guarantee that the board stays in touch with the needs and desires of the congregation.

But putting people with a representative mindset on your board or staff also carries with it some significant negatives. Here are a few examples.

- Representatives are more likely to see themselves as lobbyists for a specific constituency. Chris may become the champion of the longtime members, while Leif defends the youth. Meanwhile, Erica fights for the rights of the Sunday school, and Tim champions the need for community outreach and missions.
- Representative-oriented teams also have a harder time reaching consensus when faced with a controversial issue. By definition, representatives seek to protect their constituency. The result is often a stalemate rather than a solution.
- Finally, representative-oriented boards find it more difficult to justify keeping anyone off the board. If the primary role of a board member is to carry out the wishes of the congregation, who is to say that someone nominated by the congregation isn't qualified to be on the board?

For these reasons, and more, I'm a strong advocate of selecting board and staff members who are leadership oriented. They don't have to be aggressive, charge-the-hill leaders. But they do need the ability to think in terms of leading the congregation where God wants it to go. And that mindset is very different from worrying about every minority opinion or asking for an opinion poll on the front end of every significant decision.

Don't forget, when the elders of Israel used an opinion poll to determine which way to go, they ended up wasting forty years in the desert.

So what distinguishes a leadership-oriented team from a representative-oriented team? Here are a couple of key things to keep in mind.

No "Theys" Allowed

Leadership-oriented teams don't succumb to the tyranny of the "theys."

When I came to North Coast, our board leaned heavily to the representative side of the scale. As a result, whenever we dealt with a controversial issue, we spent a great deal of time discussing an apparently large and influential group of people known as "they." No one seemed to know who they were, and those who did seem to know weren't too keen on identifying them. But boy, did they have clout. It seemed to me that they were the largest power block in the church.

As a result, before making decisions, we spent hours worrying how "they" might respond. And afterward, we second-guessed ourselves whenever someone reported, "I've been talking to some people about this, and they have some real concerns."

To make matters worse, I could never find out who "they" were, or how many of them there were. It was strange. For a group as large and powerful as they appeared to be, they sure valued their anonymity.

Finally, I'd had enough. I told the board that as far as I was concerned, the "theys" no longer existed. I'd happily listen to comments and critiques from people with real names and faces. But nebulous theys who didn't want their identity known and hypothetical theys we couldn't identify would no longer have any sway.

The board agreed. So we instituted a "no theys" rule. It immediately pulled the rug out from underneath the biggest group of resisters we had and eventually exposed them to be a tiny minority (and at times, a mere figment of our imagination).

Our "no theys" rule applies not only to the board; it also applies to every staff meeting and to all of my dealings with the congregation. Now whenever someone says that they've been talking to some people who have a concern, I always ask, "Who are they?"

If I'm told that they wouldn't be comfortable having their names mentioned, I respond, "That's too bad, because I'm not comfortable listening to anonymous sources. Let me know when they're willing to be identified. I'll be happy to listen."

What Does God Want Us to Do?

Another mark of a leadership-oriented team is that it has a completely different agenda than a representative-oriented team. Rather than trying to figure out what everybody wants them to do, leadership teams have only one question: what does God want us to do?

I like to remind our board members and staff leaders that we're lobbyists for God. Our primary job is to listen to, discern, and carry out God's will, not the congregation's.

That's not to say that these kinds of leaders don't care about the needs and concerns of the congregation. On the contrary, good leaders are always in touch with their people. But good undershepherds never forget that they work for the Chief Shepherd, not the sheep.

If we were a representative-oriented board, I'm sure we'd still be debating the relative merits of music styles, video venues, voter guides, and new facilities. Instead, we make tough decisions and move on, even if that means losing a few people who don't agree.

Yet, ironically, the more we moved in the direction of leading rather than representing the congregation, the greater our congregational unity and support became. I'm convinced that the vast majority of people prefer to follow a healthy and united group of leaders who they know are seeking God's will rather than a bickering group of representatives, each one lobbying for his or her favorite special interest group in the church.

Insist on Spiritual Maturity

Finding leadership-oriented people is important. But it's even more important to find folks who meet the Bible's minimum requirements for *spiritual* leadership.

In many churches, the primary spiritual qualification for serving on the board or church leadership team seems to be a willing heart. Anyone who faithfully supports the church and works hard eventually finds himself or herself rewarded with a place on the team. While I know of no church that claims this as their method of selection, I know of plenty where that is exactly the way things are done.

But passages such as Acts 6, 1 Timothy 3, Titus 1, and 1 Peter 5 make it clear that a willing heart is not enough. While not everyone will agree on the exact interpretation and application of each passage, one thing is certain: the New Testament church considered spiritual maturity to be a *minimum* qualification for leadership.

By spiritual maturity, I mean a life that consistently exhibits the character of Jesus Christ. You'll also notice that all of these passages describe qualifications that focus on character — not giftedness, not biblical knowledge, not zeal. And that shouldn't surprise us, since some of the most divisive and self-centered people in our churches are those who are highly gifted, know the Bible inside out, and exhibit a zeal that puts the rest of us to shame. They just happen to also be jerks.

One word of caution when it comes to applying these biblical standards to real-life situations: we need to strike a balance between two extremes. The first extreme is to interpret these passages with such a high standard that no one can match up. (I recall a pastor telling me that in his church of more than five hundred people, no one except he and another ordained minister were qualified to lead; it didn't dawn on him that this was a terrible indictment of his six years of ministry there.)

The other danger is to redefine or water down the qualifications. Too often when someone fails to match up, we look the other way. Take, for instance, a board member whose family is falling apart. We'll offer sympathy and support, or maybe gossip, but we'll seldom ask them to step down despite multiple passages that teach that a good home life is a necessary qualification for church leadership.[6]

The same thing goes for those who are contentious, self-willed, materialistic, or hotheaded. Even if they have great gifts, knowledge, and leadership skills, they don't belong in ministry, be it on the board or the staff.

Be especially leery of those who are angry and argumentative for all the right things, particularly the single-issue crusader. I call these people pit bulls for Jesus. You know the type. They're passionate and angry against sin and sinners. To most Christians, they look like on-fire spiritual heroes. But they're not.

The apostle Paul didn't make a mistake when he warned against putting quarrelsome people into leadership.[7] And he didn't distinguish between those who are quarrelsome for the right things and those who fight over the wrong things. He simply said to keep contentious people out of leadership.

Here's why. Pit bulls bite. It's what they do. If you allow one on your board or ministry staff, don't be shocked when at some point of disagreement they turn around and bite you — and bite hard. It's what pit bulls do.

Insist on Philosophical Alignment

Still another important thing to look for when choosing leaders is philosophical alignment. By that I mean agreement with your basic philosophy of ministry and the direction that God has called your church to take.

Just because people are spiritually mature doesn't mean they'll work well together. Paul and Barnabas were both spiritual giants. But they had mutually exclusive plans for dealing with John Mark. Eventually they split up and went their separate ways, and it wasn't pretty. The Greek word used to describe their parting refers to a sharp and nasty dispute.[8] It was basically a church split.

That's why it's important to have philosophical qualifications as well as spiritual ones. Not that every potential board or staff member has to be in total agreement with everything we've previously decided or done. But they do need to be in agreement with the basic thrust of our ministry. Otherwise, conflict is inevitable.

When I first began to advocate this principle, I ran into some strong resistance, particularly in regard to our elder board. Some folks in our church couldn't understand why we would ever want to keep a spiritually mature person off the board simply because that person disagreed with our current direction of ministry.

But think about it. What business could run well with divergent business philosophies among the members of the company's board of directors? What parachurch organization could succeed with a leadership team or staff championing competing agendas and goals? And what pulpit committee would ignore alignment with the vision of the church and look only for spiritual maturity and pastoral gifts when selecting a new pastor?

Philosophical alignment matters. Those who ignore it pay a high price in conflict and in a constant revisiting of the vision God has already given. Rather than spending their time finding the best way to fulfill God's vision, they end up in endless discussions of whether or not it's God's vision in the first place. And in the meantime, the ministry languishes.

Think Through Team Fit

A final grid to use when guarding the gate is team fit. This has two aspects.

1. How will this person fit with the team *relationally*?
2. How will this person fit with the needs of the team *organizationally*?

Relational fit is easy to figure out. Is this person likable? Do they listen? Can they work well with others or only alone? Most of us know the answer quickly and intuitively. But for some reason, in church circles we tend to ignore the obvious. The most common breakdown I see in terms of relational fit happens when we allow superior Bible knowledge or spiritual zeal to trump an obvious and serious lack of social skills or a bristly personality.

Allowing this to happen is always a mistake. When board members or staff members lack social skills or, worse, don't like one another, it's hard to get much done.

Organizational fit can be a bit harder to figure out. That's because the needs of the team are always changing. At various times, we've needed completely different kinds of people on our board and on our staff. Just as a basketball team could never win with the NBA's five best point guards or centers, a ministry team sometimes needs a particular skill or mindset to balance or to deal with current realities so that they can move on to the next level.

For instance, one year we came down to two potential board members who were both qualified spiritually and in every other way. We chose the more extroverted member because we had mostly introverts on the board. Another time, we chose the person who was newest to the church because we already had many long-term members. Still another time, we asked who could best help us navigate the growing complexity that came with our growth.

In each case, spiritual qualifications came first and philosophical alignment came second. But after that, team fit helped us make the final call.

Good Enough Probably Isn't

When it comes to hiring staff members, one of the most common mistakes that pastors and boards make is to fill the position with the best person available. While that may sound like a logical approach, it's a recipe for a losing team.

Here's what happens. Fearing a long-term vacancy more than choosing the wrong person, we collect résumés, hold extensive interviews, and then hire the best person we can find, even though we have lingering doubts that this is the right person for the job.

I've hired a couple people this way and deeply regretted it each time. In each case, an exhaustive search came up empty. So we went back to the drawing board and changed the criteria. We hired the best person available, knowing they weren't ideal. We figured they'd rise to the occasion (despite no supporting evidence) and we'd find a way to adjust to their shortcomings. As for the lack of chemistry and connectedness, we blew that off too, assuming that given enough time we'd all learn to connect and work well together.

It never happened.

I've since learned that if the *best person available* is not the *right person for the job*, it's far better to have a long-term vacancy than a long-term cancer on the team — even if everyone else is hounding me to fill the position right now.

Résumés Always Look Better Than People

Jesus said it well: a prophet is always without honor in his hometown.[9] I've found the same thing holds true when it comes to hiring staff members. A résumé always looks better than the people we already know.

That's because we know their shortcomings all too well. But the truth is everyone has shortcomings, even the person on the other end of a highly polished résumé. In fact, I've found that great résumés often hide glaring weaknesses.

For instance, if this person is so great, why are they so available?

I've also found that most pastors aren't very good at interviewing strangers. We tend to like people and want to help them. So it takes a real dog to come off poorly in a random interview. Yet the gap between the person we thought we interviewed and the person they prove to be once hired is not unlike the difference between a blind date and ten years of marriage. Things have a tendency to work out a little differently than we first expected.

That's why, whenever possible, I prefer to hire and promote from within. If neither of these are possible, I prefer to hire from existing webs of relationship. These folks are known entities. When they speak, I not only know what they say; I also know what they mean. In the case of someone who is already on our staff or in the church, I know they get our DNA. And in the case of a layperson joining the staff, I know they chose our church. They aren't a mercenary; they're a raving fan.

Obviously, sometimes you can't hire from within. When we hit five or six thousand in attendance, some ministry areas were too large and complex for someone to make the jump from being an intern to leading a major department. We had to go outside.

But when we did our success rate dropped precipitously. On inside hires, we had nearly a 100 percent hit rate, and the same for those that we recruited out of previous working relationships and friendships.

But outside résumé-hires were a different matter. Our success rate dropped to around 70 percent. Not bad for blind dates, but not too good when it comes to building a healthy ministry team.

Character Is More Important Than Giftedness

A final lesson I've learned about guarding the gate is that character is always more important than giftedness. Just as in sports, the best players don't win championships; the best team does.

Don't get me wrong. I want the best players possible. But given the choice between a prickly high-performance staff member and a steady team builder, I'll choose the team builder every time. Over the long haul, they'll outperform the prima donna, guaranteed.

Here's why. Whenever a staff member's giftedness and platform surpass their character, it eventually creates disillusionment and cynicism among those they work with. It also tends to create festering jealousies and division among the rest of the staff, especially among those who become frustrated and disheartened by all the success and public praise they see heaped on someone they know is actually a jerk behind the scenes.

No matter how skilled someone is, no matter how large their area of ministry becomes, no matter how amazing their portfolio, eventually the curtain will be pulled back. True character will poke out. It's inevitable.

That's why if I have *any* doubts or if there is *any* aspect of a person's personality or life that I hope people won't see, I'll slam the gate shut. Ignoring lingering doubts or character flaws in a potential team member in the hope that no one else will notice is a foolish pipe dream. It won't happen. Great skills and giftedness in what someone does can never counterbalance a fatal flaw in who they are. That's why guarding the gate is one of the most important things I do.

Chapter 4

What Game Are We Playing?

How Growth Changes Everything

NEVER FORGET, GROWTH CHANGES everything. A storefront church, a midsized church, a large church, and a megachurch aren't simply bigger versions of the same thing. They are completely different animals. They have little in common, especially relationally, organizationally, and structurally.

It's not that one is better than the other. It's just that they're different. Leadership teams that fail to recognize or adapt to these differences inevitably experience unnecessary conflict or shrink back to a congregational size that best fits the structures and patterns they cling to.

I learned this the hard way. Upon arriving at North Coast Church, I helped set up a system of governance, leadership structures, and staff relationships tailored to our church and current size. I even had Bible verses to back everything up.

But what I didn't know was that I had inadvertently put us in an organizational straitjacket. After a rocky start, we experienced years of steady and healthy growth. Then suddenly, the systems, structures, and patterns that had previously fueled our growth stopped working. Worse, they began to constrict and choke off the very health and innovation they had been created to foster.

What happened?

I had failed to realize that *growth changes everything.*

What had worked so well in the past no longer fit as the size of our staff and number of our ministries increased. But since I had tacked a Bible verse onto everything, any changes I made seemed like a change in my theology and values — and they were resisted as such. So I tried to downplay the changes, either ignoring them or pretending they weren't happening.

It didn't work.

Everyone knew things were different. We just didn't know why, or what to do about it.

Most of the time, we worked our way through these transitions with a little whitewater followed by smooth sailing. But there was one time when we almost didn't make it. Unlike the low-level frustrations of the past, this one erupted into a full-scale attempted coup. It turned ugly fast.

Frankly, I never saw it coming. We were in the middle of a strong growth spurt and one of the best evangelistic years we'd ever had. I thought we were on a roll. I had no idea we were rolling downhill, headed straight for a cliff.

It all broke loose when a couple of longtime staff members, deeply grieved over the loss of influence and relationships these changes had brought, approached the board and in no uncertain terms suggested that I was losing it spiritually and emotionally. They requested that I be sent away for a few weeks or months to get fixed at one of those retreat centers for burned-out pastors. In the meantime, they'd take over and run things until I got back.

It was a mess. I remember at one point lying in bed and telling my wife, Nancy, that we probably needed to think about leaving. I wasn't up to tearing down what God had built up just to win a power struggle, even if it was one I could win. I knew the collateral damage in the lives of innocent people would be too great.

Our board jumped in and for the next couple of weeks tried to figure out what was going on. (Fortunately, knowledge of the conflict was limited to a handful of staff members and the board; the congregation had no idea what was going on behind the scenes.)

To the board's credit, they didn't jump to my defense. In fact, it was quite the opposite. Realizing that smoke usually means fire, they at first assumed the problem was mine. But as they investigated further, they came to the conclusion that the whole thing was nothing more than "workplace baloney."

They told the ringleaders that I wasn't going anywhere, authorized a few significant changes in our reporting structures, and reaffirmed their confidence in my leadership. One of the aggrieved parties left. The other one acquiesced. To my surprise, in the next few months, things quickly returned to normal — even most of the broken relationships were significantly restored.

The board's initial courage to confront and challenge me, and their eventual wisdom in navigating the crisis, reflects well on the principles found in these pages. Faced with a major and confusing crisis, they were neither yes-men nor adversaries. They were wise elders — carefully selected, well trained, and ready to make a tough call when necessary.

As things were calming down, I began to seek the Lord for some word pictures to help me better understand and explain what had happened. I knew that despite all the "sin words" that both sides had thrown around ("arrogant," "self-willed," "unaccountable," "not a team player," "boundary queen," and "inflexible," to name a few), the real issue was not sin so much as the deep hurt and discomfort that came with our changing organizational dynamics. But I didn't know how to explain this in ways that could help us or others avoid falling into the same trap all over again.

Then one day while journaling about the situation, I noticed something I'd never seen before. The changes we had to work through at each stage of growth resembled the changes an athlete must make every time he or she switches from playing one sport to another. With each change in the sports calendar, an athlete has to adapt to significant alterations in everything from the rules of the game to the roles, relationships, and even equipment used. I saw that the same thing holds true for leadership teams in any growing church or organization. Growth produces predictable changes in the way leaders and leadership teams relate and carry out their functions, changes that are remarkably parallel to the changes an athlete must go through to transition from running track to playing golf, basketball, or football.

Here's what I mean.

The Track Star

The solo pastor or leader can be compared to a track star. Like the high jumper or sprinter, the solo pastor may work out with others, but he performs alone, often without fanfare or support and usually before a small crowd peppered with close family and friends.

This solo role is unique and challenging. On the upside, it offers tremendous freedom. Independent types love it. On the downside, it can be overwhelming and lonely. Finances can be a constant struggle.

Perhaps that's why most of the solo pastors and leaders I've known look forward to someday being a part of a team, so much so that they often end up pulling together a group of lay leaders or close friends to create a sense of teamwork and shared ministry as soon as possible.

Golfing Buddies

The next stage of a leadership team is best illustrated by the game of golf. The dynamics of a small group of leaders are very similar to those found among a small group of golfing buddies.

Golf is a highly relational game. So are small ministry teams. Golf is most enjoyable when played with friends. And while it's preferable to have similar skills, a stroke a hole is no big deal. The leisurely pace allows for extended conversation and camaraderie. In fact, it's a major part of the game. Afterward, everyone hangs around for a snack and a drink while analyzing the last round and planning the next one.

For the highly relational pastor, a golf-sized staff or leadership team is often the most enjoyable stage of ministry. The relationships tend to be deep, the sharing is genuine, and the concern for one another goes far beyond the golf course. Doing what you like with people you like is hard to beat.

The Basketball Team

When a ministry team grows larger, the relationships and functions begin to resemble those on a basketball team far more than anything you'd find on a golf course.

Basketball is primarily a team sport, not a friendship sport. It requires working together, trusting one another, and sharing the ball. But unlike golfing buddies, members of a basketball team don't expect that everyone will be best friends. There are too many players for that.

That doesn't mean quality relationships are no longer important. It just means they are different. While basketball teams seldom share the same camaraderie found on the golf course, the good teams still have excellent esprit de corps. The locker room is small and intimate. Everyone rides to the game on one bus. Trash-talking is half the fun.

But the roles and relationships on the basketball court are no longer as egalitarian as those found on the golf course. Winning basketball teams have both role players and stars. The stars take the clutch shots. They're given more freedom to freelance. They're paid more. Yet a basketball team can't win without role players. Too many self-identified stars and just one basketball is a formula for a losing team.

One thing, however, doesn't change at this stage. Everyone is still aware of what everyone else is doing. Like golfers, all the members of a basketball team watch every play. When the coach addresses the team, he speaks to everyone. Most players can play multiple positions, so asking someone to change roles for the good of the team is no big deal. It's often done in the middle of the game if someone gets into foul trouble.

For many entrepreneurial leaders, the basketball stage is especially rewarding because it retains much of the relational connection found on the golf course while adding the ego satisfaction of playing before a much bigger crowd in a larger arena.

The Football Team

When a leadership team (be it the board and staff or the ministry staff alone) increases to fifteen or twenty-five members, and in some cases fifty, one hundred, or more, the game changes radically. It starts to feel and function more like a football team.

This change can be very unsettling for those who prefer golf or basketball. And for those who still *think* they're playing golf or basketball, it can be downright dangerous.

Football is a game of highly specialized roles. It's so complex that even the coach has to watch the films before he knows what happened. Few players are interchangeable. Guards seldom become quarterbacks. Teamwork is more important than one-on-one skill. In fact, a great athlete who insists on continually freelancing can mess up the entire offense or defense.

The same holds true for a larger leadership team. At this stage, it's no longer possible for everyone to know or have input on what everyone else is doing. Unlike their counterparts on the golf course or basketball court, football players don't know, and don't expect to know, what everyone else is up to. The offensive and defensive teams have completely different game plans and playbooks. When not in the game, football players don't watch the game; they huddle with their unit and position coach to plan for the next series of plays. The offensive line doesn't complain when the defense adds a new blitz package without telling them about it. They're just glad somebody finally got to the quarterback.

It's also harder to maintain camaraderie on a football team because of the number of players and their distinctly different roles. While golfing buddies enjoy long, leisurely lunches and a basketball team goes everywhere together, a football team is divided into offense and defense and takes two buses to the game. Some teammates hardly know one another.

For the members of a leadership team that once played golf or basketball together, this stage of growth can be an especially difficult adjustment. Team members who are used to being in on everything may feel insignificant, left out, and no longer a vital part of the team, which explains why key board members and staff members who once rejoiced over the idea of growth and helped produce it may suddenly turn sour when growth actually happens. They don't like the new rules and patterns of relationship that come with playing the new game.

As a ministry grows, some players won't be able to make the change. Some won't want to. But there is nothing you or they can do about it. At this size, the game has changed. The only question is whether they will put on the pads or just stand there and get run over.

Caught by Surprise

While these relational and functional changes are inevitable in a growing leadership team, many leaders don't see them coming or don't realize that they've already taken place. It reminds me of a fellow I played basketball with in high school.

Todd, a star football player and good athlete, decided to go out for the varsity basketball team. He made the team. But whenever it came time to play hard-nosed defense, he reverted to the tactics he'd learned on the football field. He never quite understood that this was a new game with new rules.

What Todd, the football player, called "a little pushing and shoving," the basketball referees called "a foul." Soon Todd was on the bench, confused and frustrated that the officials didn't appreciate the tight defense that had won him awards as a cornerback.

Time for Change

The most obvious indicator that the game has changed and that leadership roles and relationships need to change is the number of people on your team. But there are two other indicators that strongly suggest the game is changing, even if no one has yet noticed: relational overload and increased miscommunication.

Relational Overload

The first sign that the game may have changed is a significant increase in the time spent massaging relationships. Whenever conflict significantly or suddenly increases, absent a major crisis or controversial decision, it usually means that the game has changed and some of the key players never got the memo.

I remember the first time that happened at North Coast. My preferred style of leadership is relational. I'd rather convince you than give you a directive. I don't do memorandums. Instead, I like to pass on vision and direction through ad hoc meetings around the watercooler, in the hallway, or over lunch.

My relational style worked well for a long while, especially in my track-star and golf-buddy days. But when we moved from golf to basketball, we had to schedule a weekly staff meeting and make sure it actually happened. Though it felt a little artificial, it was no big deal. At this stage, we hit our stride. We hummed along for a decade. It was a blast. Everyone was happy. The church grew. We joked about being a "black hole" because no one who joined the team ever left.

But along with our steady growth in attendance came a constant need to add new staff. Eventually, we were no longer the size of an overgrown basketball team. We were a football team. No one noticed, however, because the new staff members joined the team one at a time, though I did wonder why I was spending a lot more time trying to keep everyone happy and in the loop.

I slowly found myself being sucked into a relational nightmare. Since most of the ministry team thought we were still playing basketball, they were upset any time something happened without their knowledge or input. Since I also thought we were still playing basketball, I assumed their complaints were legitimate. I'd spend hours each week trying to catch up with everyone who missed a meeting or wanted to have input. Time to reflect, lead, and study was squeezed into the late evenings and early mornings. Days off became days to catch up. What had once been an energizing ministry became a dreaded job.

Only when I realized that I couldn't play basketball with a football team did I find my way out of this nightmare.

Increased Miscommunication

A second sign that the game may have changed is a marked increase in miscommunication. When important messages are chronically missed or misunderstood, it's time to change the way we play the game.

In a golf sized team, communication is easy and natural. Seldom is there a need to set up a special meeting to discuss something, since you're already together most of the time.

That's why when our staff was small, we hardly ever scheduled a meeting. It felt silly to do so. If we had something to discuss, we did it on the spot. It was fun and fluid. It took little time or planning. But as our ministry staff grew, someone was always missing, either out of town, on vacation, or in a meeting somewhere else. Our preferred style of ad hoc and informal communication no longer worked, and we had to make our meetings more structured and intentional.

It reminds me of something I learned while coaching my son's youth-league basketball teams. Occasionally, another team would throw us a surprise defense or press. The solution was rather simple. But nothing was harder than trying to explain it to the entire team in the middle of a game.

The information itself was not that complicated. All I needed was a chalkboard and about two minutes to explain what was happening and how to respond. But in the hecticness of a timeout, there was always one kid who would misunderstand what I said, tune out, or otherwise not get the message. Inevitably, the team would go back on the court and continue to turn the ball over. But in the structured calm of halftime or our next practice, what was impossible to do in the chaos of the game was easy to do in the calm of a special meeting.

It's the same with a leadership team; the larger the team gets and the more hectic the game becomes, the greater the need for special meetings, chalk talks, and film sessions to get and then keep everyone on the same page.

However, the changeover to a more structured pattern of meetings and communication is not always easy. Expect some significant resistance.

Duffers who thrive on leisurely fairway talks will feel cheated when you substitute rambling conversations with scripted meetings or agendas. For many of them, it's not the game but the relationships that they love most.

Basketball players accustomed to knowing everything about the game plan are seldom thrilled when a new structure leaves them focused on only part of the picture. After all, in most organizations, knowledge holds the key to power and prestige.

Because of this, and because some folks will always like the old game better than the new game no matter what, every leader of a growing organization faces enormous pressure to keep or revert to the old ways of leading and communicating, even when they no longer work. Lots of people prefer the familiarity and comfort of the past, even at the expense of the future and the success of the mission. It's human nature.

That can make it tempting to go back, especially when longtime board or staff members pine for the good old days. But don't do it. It never works. It might make a few folks happier, but the rest of the team will flounder, and it won't be long until your ministry shrinks back to a size appropriate to the structures, relational patterns, and communication style they've convinced you to use.

Why These Changes Sneak Up on Us

The need to change the game, as well as the rules of the game, tends to sneak up on leaders and leadership teams because growth exponentially increases complexity. We might think that we've only *added* a couple of new programs or staff members, but in reality, we've *multiplied* organizational complexity and the lines of communication that need to be maintained.

For instance, some years ago, I added a new member to a key ministry team. Previously, this team functioned like a well-oiled machine. We made great decisions. We enjoyed the process. But the moment this new person came aboard, things fell apart. A group that once reached consensus quickly and easily began debating every little detail. Minor coalitions formed; relationships suffered.

Our once enjoyable strategy sessions became dreaded staff meetings.

What happened? We had added one player too many without changing the rules. Like the proverbial straw that breaks the camel's back, the newest member of the team pushed our meetings to relational overload.

Look what happens every time a new board member, staff member, or program is added to your ministry mix. The lines of communication and the degrees of complexity increase exponentially.

> 2 people or programs = 2 lines of communication
> 3 people or programs = 6 lines of communication
> 4 people or programs = 12 lines of communication
> 5 people or programs = 20 lines of communication
> 6 people or programs = 30 lines of communication

By the time you get to 20 people or programs, you have 380 lines of communication to manage!

Unfortunately, this is a principle that few leaders or leadership teams understand until it's too late. Yet I've found that simply being aware of the tremendous complexity that comes with every additional program and team member goes a long way toward preparing me and our team for the changes that come with growth. Just seeing this list of increased complexity has sometimes been all it takes to get a board member or staff member to realize and accept that the game has to change even if they don't want it to.

As a youth, I played sports year-round. I certainly had a favorite. But once a particular season began, it didn't matter which one I liked the best (or which one came most naturally). All that mattered was that I was willing to set aside the equipment and rules of the old game in exchange for the equipment and rules of the game I was currently playing. In hindsight, that was great training for leadership and ministry.

Too often, organizations and leaders insist on playing with the equipment, rules, and regulations they are most comfortable with, even when the game has changed completely. It's a tough way to lead. The odds of success are about the same as for the world's greatest golfer to drop a five-foot putt with a basketball. Some things won't happen, no matter how hard we try or how talented we may be.

In contrast, successful leaders and healthy organizations play the game that's in season. They accept the new conditions and rules. They discern what kind of leadership is needed and adjust their structures, roles, and relationships accordingly.

And then they play ball!

Chapter 5

Six Things Every Leadership Team Needs to Know

Axioms to Lead By

WHEN IT COMES TO leadership, some of the most widely believed and broadly disseminated axioms of conventional wisdom are pure baloney. They're like classic urban legends. They sound plausible, but upon further examination, they don't hold up.

These faulty ideas have resulted in countless well-intentioned but poor decisions, especially when it comes to planning, evaluating, and creating new ministries. I've found that one of the best ways to confront these myths is to make sure that all of my board members, staff members, and pastors understand what I like to call "Six Things Every Leadership Team Needs to Know."

I'll warn you ahead of time: many of these concepts are counterintuitive, a bit like asking someone to turn into a skid. But they will enable your lay leaders and staff to make wiser decisions and avoid the pitfalls that derail so many ministry teams.

My list of the six things I want every one of my leaders to know:

1. Ignore your weaknesses
2. Surveys are a waste of time

3. Seek permission, not buy-in
4. Let squeaky wheels squeak
5. Let dying programs die
6. Plan in pencil

1. Ignore Your Weaknesses

Focusing on organizational weakness leaves little time or energy for maximizing strengths. It puts everyone on the defensive. And while it may result in a ministry with few major flaws, it will also produce one without any major strengths.

Think about the way most of us have been taught to evaluate the spirituality and health of a church. The process often goes something like this:

1. Size up the ministry
2. Identify any major weaknesses
3. Develop and implement a plan for removing those weaknesses

That may seem like a rational approach, but it violates one of the most important paradoxes of church leadership: *successful ministries ignore their weaknesses and focus on their strengths.*

That's not to say that every weakness should be ignored. But most should. And it's not to say that wise leaders are unaware of their weaknesses. On the contrary, they are very aware of them. But wise leaders and leadership teams understand that unless a weakness is potentially fatal, it's usually a waste of time and energy to worry too much about it. It's far better to focus on islands of strength and build on them.

It reminds me of a church I once knew that was unable to acquire a permanent worship facility because of the high cost of California real estate. The leaders were convinced that their single greatest weakness was their lack of adequate facilities, and they were right. So for the next ten years, the pastor and board focused all of their excess time, money, and emotional energy on finding a permanent facility.

Unfortunately, they couldn't find one.

In the meantime, they failed to develop and build on their two greatest strengths: First, they were blessed with a lot of young singles and families who were willing and eager to try new things (as evidenced by their attendance at a church with such terrible facilities). These folks would have quickly accepted many new and innovative programs that would have taken years to launch in a more traditional setting. Second, the absence of a large mortgage left them in excellent financial shape. Most years, they ended up well in the black. That meant they had the money to hire a top-quality staff. But because they were so dialed in on their facility problem, they stashed all their excess cash into a building fund.

So instead of a top-notch staff and the great ministry they would have produced, the church settled for a well-paid senior pastor and a group of poorly paid, not-very-good part-time assistants in order to save up enough money to someday fix what they perceived to be their big problem.

The result was a ministry that never went anywhere. The last time I talked to the pastor, he was still bemoaning his plight and his facility problem. It never dawned on him how many other ministries in California had started and succeeded in those ten years despite having the same problem.

The difference? The successful ministries were unconcerned about their inadequate facilities. They spent all their energy maximizing their strengths and opportunities.

That's the way it is with strong churches. They are almost always opportunity-centered. They don't fixate on, "What are we not very good at?" They ask, "What are we doing uncommonly well? And how can we get better at it?"

2. Surveys Are a Waste of Time

Another way that leadership teams get sidetracked is when they depend on surveys to plan their ministry. Surveys are to leadership teams what butterflies are to Little League right fielders. They quickly take our eye off the ball, and they have nothing to do with the game at hand.

The problem is that *surveys (especially anonymous surveys) seldom give us the accurate information we think we're getting.*

People tend to answer with what they perceive to be the right answer. When asked about food, most people will say they're making an effort to count calories, avoid fats, and eat more vegetables. But the reality is that we're buying more red meat and fast food than ever.

It reminds me of the time I surveyed a church to find their level of interest in small groups. I was thrilled to discover that over half the congregation said they wanted to be in one. But when it came time to sign up, only a handful did. They felt they ought to be in a Bible study, so they had checked the yes box. But their answers had nothing to do with their actual behavior.

That's how surveys work.

A second major problem with surveys and marketing studies is that they almost always reject innovation. We can evaluate a new idea or program only by comparing it with something we're already familiar with. Since it doesn't yet exist, we tend to give answers that have nothing to do with how we'll respond once we see the real deal.

That's what happened when market researchers studied the potential interest in minivans, microwave ovens, fax machines, FedEx, PC networks, and cable television. They got it completely wrong because the people they surveyed had no idea what these things would actually look like or do. So they said they'd never buy one.

Fortunately, Lee Iacocca wanted his minivan, Bill Gates wanted his PC, and the Japanese decided to manufacture and ship boatloads of fax machines and microwaves anyway. They all made a ton of money, while the MBAs and market researchers whose surveys convinced everyone else that these were all bad ideas ended up with egg on their face.

The same thing happens when a board or staff insists on surveying congregational interest in a genuinely new program, idea, or innovation. People won't (and can't) answer in terms of how they will actually respond. They have no idea since they haven't experienced it yet.

A third major problem with surveys is that when asked what should be offered, most of us answer in terms of what we want, not what we need (and even then, many of us don't really know what we want).

Ask any group of Christians what they want to study next, and invariably you'll find prophecy and a host of controversial subjects near the top of the list. Yet teaching on prophecy is hardly most people's greatest need. And most of those who tell us they want to study prophecy really just want to know who the Antichrist is. Once they discover that we're on Jesus' welcoming committee, not his programming committee, they bail out — usually by the third week or so.

There is, however, one type of quasi survey that does make sense. It's what I call "running the magnet through the sand." It's the process of asking volunteers to find out who wants to help launch or pioneer a new initiative. Unlike traditional surveys, this isn't asking the larger group what they *think* of an idea or program; it's asking if anyone wants to *help* launch it.

The response to this type of question or survey will let you know if there are any early adopters ready to jump aboard. It's usually a good indicator of whether something has a chance of getting off the ground. But this type of survey, designed to capture the names of early adopters, is a far cry from a traditional survey designed to find out what everyone wants, thinks, or feels.

3. Seek Permission, Not Buy-In

Leaders and leadership teams can easily get sidetracked by the endless pursuit of buy-in. The reason for this is also one reason we overuse surveys and polls: we're looking for a way to get everyone aboard.

Certainly, leaders and leadership teams need broad buy-in for their current mission and methods of ministry. But when it comes to setting a new direction or starting new initiatives, it's seldom needed. *Buy-in is overrated. Most of the time, we don't need buy-in as much as we need permission.*

Buy-in is usually defined as having the support of most, if not all, of the key stakeholders (and virtually all of the congregation). It takes a ton of time to get. It's incredibly elusive.

Permission, on the other hand, is relatively easy to acquire, even from those who think your idea is loony and bound to fail. That's because permission simply means, "I'll let you try it," as opposed to buy-in, which means, "I'll back your play."

I've found that most people will grant the pastor, board, or staff permission to try something new as long as they don't have to make personal changes or express agreement with the idea.

For instance, when we started our first video-venue worship service in 1998, most of the staff and the congregation thought it was a nutty idea. They'd never seen one before, and no one else in the country had yet started one. All they could imagine was a glorified overflow room, and we all know what an overflow room is: it's punishment for being late. They couldn't imagine anyone choosing to go to one.

Frankly, if I had believed the buy-in myth (or if our board had), I'd still be trying to convince everyone that video cafés can work. And they'd still think I'm nuts. But since all I asked for was permission to try it, I got the okay; as long as their names weren't on it, they didn't have to sell it or go to it, and it didn't cost too much money.

Needless to say, on this side of the multisite revolution, video venues proved to be a good idea. But the key to getting it off the ground was my willingness (and that of our board and staff) to settle for permission rather than buy-in.

In essence, I was doing something I learned from Lyle Schaller decades ago: I was counting the yes votes and ignoring the no votes.

For instance, the week we launched our Video Café, 173 people chose to attend. They were my yes votes. Twenty-four months later, 1,300 adults attended! On the surface, that sounds like a smashing success. But in reality, that first weekend over 3,185 people voted no by not coming. Imagine if my board or staff had insisted that we have broad buy-in from all of them before launching. We'd still be lobbying.

Yet that's how many boards and staffs evaluate a new initiative. Before giving their okay, they want proof positive that the idea will work and that everyone is in line and ready to charge the hill. But if an idea or program is really new and innovative, there will never be enough evidence to "prove" that it will work. After all, it's never been done before. And that's what makes buy-in almost impossible to gain.

Another significant advantage that comes from not worrying too much about buy-in is that it makes failure far more palatable. Permission not only gets things up and running much faster; it also makes it much easier to close up shop when a great idea proves to be a dumb idea. Since nobody thought it would work in the first place, few chips are lost, and most people will let you try something else again next time.

But if everyone is pumped up and the buy-in is broad, failure becomes a big deal. The more that a new program, ministry direction, or innovation has been pushed, sold, and championed, the higher the cost in lost credibility if it fails to fly. And the greater the resistance the next time you want to try something new or different.

4. Let Squeaky Wheels Squeak

Spiritual leaders are called to care for all the flock, but one group of people is best treated with benign neglect. I call these folks "squeaky wheels."

You'll find them in every church, sometimes on the fringe, other times sneaking into staff and lay leadership roles. But unlike other people with occasional legitimate complaints and criticisms, squeaky wheels are never quite happy, and they make sure everybody knows it.

The natural response of most leaders and leadership teams is to oil these squeaky wheels. We alter our plans or give these folks extra attention in the hope of silencing their criticism. Unfortunately, it seldom works. Most squeaky wheels keep right on squeaking, for one simple reason: they don't squeak for a lack of oil; they squeak because it's their nature to squeak.

Wise pastors and leadership teams know an important paradox of leadership: *church harmony is inversely related to the amount of time spent oiling squeaky wheels.*

This is a lesson I was slow to grasp. In my zeal for maintaining peace and unity within the body and for holding on to everyone who came, I allowed a tiny group of chronic complainers to have an inordinate impact on our decisions and ministry.

So did our board. In effect, we gave squeaky wheels a seat at the leadership table and veto power over anything they didn't like.

One man, whom I'll call Matt, held a pivotal up-front role in the early days of our ministry. He was good at what he did. I couldn't imagine what we'd do without him. But I also couldn't imagine how any one person could have so much angst and negativity.

Whether it was our song selection, a program change, my preaching content, or our budget, Matt was always uptight about something. Every time I talked to him, I came away emotionally exhausted. Even when he didn't have an issue to complain about, he always knew someone else who did.

Listening to him, you would have thought our church was on the edge of disaster, with large segments of people ready to leave. For nearly three years, I tried everything I could think of to keep him happy and placate his "the sky is falling" fears. Nothing worked. But I kept after it because I feared losing him, especially in light of his up-front worship skills.

We were a small, struggling congregation. Even though Matt's moodiness was legend, most people in the congregation genuinely liked him. I did too, when he wasn't driving me nuts. Over the years, he and his wife had helped a number of younger couples through rough waters. He had a lot of chips stored up, or so I thought. I feared how people would react if he got too upset or if, heaven forbid, he left the church. I wondered if they'd all leave too.

My mistake (and the board's) was assuming that it was possible to keep a squeaky wheel happy. I failed to realize that some people will be unhappy no matter what.

Finally, in the middle of a discussion of how to handle his latest grievance, one of our board members asked why we didn't just take him up on it the next time he threatened to resign. To my surprise, the rest of the board chimed in with their agreement.

So I did it.

Sure enough, Matt and his wife soon left the church. But the music crisis I dreaded never materialized. We found someone of nearly equal talent almost immediately. As for Matt's influence, that too was overblown. No one else left the church, and only four or five people even mentioned his departure.

The fact is, oiling squeaky wheels can be hazardous to your church's health. Leaders who place too much emphasis on keeping squeaky wheels happy risk abdicating leadership. Instead of initiating, the leaders end up reacting. Instead of asking, "What does God want us to do?" they ask, "How will the squeaky wheels react?"

It also sends an unspoken message to the rest of the congregation. It tells everyone that the best way to have influence around here is to complain, and the louder and more often you complain, the more power you'll have. It's no wonder, then, that leadership teams that try to oil squeaky wheels end up having the most wheels to oil.

5. Let Dying Programs Die

Another counterintuitive principle that leadership teams often ignore is the importance of letting dying programs die. Programs that are terminally ill need to be put out of their misery ASAP.

Abandonment is to the future what tilling the soil is to next year's crop. It makes the future possible. It sets the stage so that the new seeds can grow without the old roots choking them out. *Without a commitment and willingness to cease funding and staffing the programs that no longer work, we'll never have enough money and energy to create the future.*

The difficulty with this principle is that every program has its champions. Even after rigor mortis has set in, someone will still champion the cause. Usually these champions are former leaders who invested time and energy into making the program successful during the good old days or the tiny remnant who believe that if just one person is helped it's worth whatever it costs.

But a leadership team can't let these people sway how resources are allocated. If we give in to everyone who pleads for heroic measures to save their favorite ministry, it won't be long until we've become a historical preservation society, so loaded with yesterday that we have no energy or resources left for today or tomorrow.

I remember once being asked to consult with a friend's small suburban church. The pastor was overwhelmed, and the board was discouraged. They were particularly concerned about a chronic lack of volunteers, which they interpreted as spiritual apathy.

I asked them to list every program and volunteer position in the church. When they were done, the problem was obvious. They had far more positions to fill than the church had actual attenders. Their problem was not a spiritually lethargic congregation; it was a proliferation of programs far beyond the church's ability to sustain them.

How had this happened? For years, the board had failed to prune even a single program. Every new ministry became a permanent fixture. Eventually the church began to drown in a sea of propped-up and outdated programs, traditions, and ministries.

As is all too common, these leaders had no understanding of the importance of planned abandonment. In fact, they saw it as heartless. When a program or ministry failed to live up to its expectations, they let it hang on in the optimistic hope that someday it would click back into gear.

Wise leaders, boards, and staffs know that they have only a limited supply of time, energy, and money. That's why they periodically stop and ask, "Why are we doing this?" If there is no good reason, they refuse to let their limited resources be wasted on outdated and ineffective ministries. They give a dead or dying program exactly what it needs: a fine Christian burial.

6. Plan in Pencil

Overly rigid planning is yet another way that leadership teams can unintentionally sabotage their ministry. I find that many pastors, board members, and staff members assume that the best-run organizations are those that have the clearest and most detailed blueprint for the future.

But the truth is that *the best-run churches and organizations are masters of the midcourse correction.* They plan in pencil. They know the power of "fuzzy and flexible plans."

Obviously, there is a time and place for highly detailed strategies and precise planning, but as a rule, the best plans are flexible and easily changed. And this is especially true in the two areas where churches tend to be most inflexible: finances and policy.

Fuzzy Budgets

Crafting the budget is often an intense and drawn-out process that begins months before it takes effect. In many churches, it's a highly detailed and restrictive document that, once adopted, can't be changed until the next year.

While the motivation to avoid fiscal irresponsibility is admirable, the cure is often worse than the disease. Because our budgets are planned so many months in advance, by the end of the fiscal year, many ministries are operating on assumptions and forecasts that were made up to fifteen months earlier. Yet there is no way to know what the income, expenditures, needs, and opportunities will be that far in advance.

That's why we've opted for a fuzzy and flexible budget. Though it's clear and detailed, we realize that the budget is nothing more than an educated guess of what we think we'll need and what we think we'll bring in. We treat it as a guide, not a straitjacket.

Over the years, this mindset has saved us lots of money and has allowed us to take advantage of countless opportunities that we would have otherwise had to pass up. When a great deal on computers, a children's playground set, flatscreen TVs for the youth buildings, or new carpet for the Video Café became available, we were able to jump on it without having to go through a belabored process that would have caused us to miss the window of opportunity. When an unbudgeted A player suddenly became available, we were able to hire him rather than ask everyone to wait until next year, when we could get it in the budget.

Opportunity never sends a text message saying it's coming. It just shows up. A flexible budget is one of the best ways to be ready when it does. Our only restrictions are that (1) we have the money, and (2) if it's a very large expense, the elder board approves the expenditure (which can be done via a quick email or phone vote).

The result of our fuzzy budgets has been a ministry free to move ahead rather than forced to wait until next year.

One caveat: I do find that we *constantly* need to remind everyone *up front* that our budget is a planning tool, not a straitjacket, that it's an estimate, not the law of the Medes and Persians. When we do that, most people seem to get it. There's very little push back. But when we forget and assume that people know or remember that our budget is fuzzy, many quickly revert to the mindset they've always known. They treat the budget as a sacred document.

Flexible Policies

Policy is another area where flexibility makes a big difference. Leadership boards and staff members who fill executive roles tend to make two mistakes when it comes to policy: (1) they have too many policies, and (2) they treat every policy as if it were a law from God himself.

Obviously, some policies need to be unbendable (for instance, insisting on background checks on everyone who works with kids). But many other policies need to be treated as general guidelines rather than rigid rules. And at no point should a policy ever be allowed to trump common sense.

Yet that's just what happens all too often.

Virtually every leadership team or staff I've worked with has had at least one or two members whose personality causes them to see everything as black and white. In many cases these same folks also have a strong bias toward risk aversion. It makes for a dangerous combination.

Putting these people in charge of anything is a big mistake. They'll kill your morale. What they see as streamlining procedures and limiting risk everyone else experiences as petty, arbitrary, and disruptive rules.

Inflexible policies are most often found in the financial arena, facility and security procedures, and reporting systems. When a church allows those who oversee these areas to put their stamp on the entire ministry, it's a case of letting the tail wag the dog. Whenever avoiding potential problems and streamlining backroom procedures becomes a ministry priority, the front line suffers.

A similar thing happens when it comes to church constitutions and bylaws. Most are far too detailed and restrictive. They often include rigid and detailed clauses that are nothing more than a pendulum-swing response to some unpleasant event in the past. They remind me of the complaint of an old navy man: "Every time a sailor does something stupid and drowns, we make a new regulation."

A far better response would be to simply have a funeral for a dumb sailor and to wait until three or four sailors die the same way before rewriting the manual. But policy types have a hard time doing that. They're petrified of being blamed if anything bad happens twice.

Overly restrictive constitutions and bylaws reveal a profound lack of trust. It's as if those who write them trust God's ability to lead in their own life but not his ability to lead in the life of the next group of leaders. So to keep future leaders from going astray, they put in all kinds of detailed regulations and procedures that make sense today but that will make no sense tomorrow.

It reminds me of one church I worked with whose constitution mandated a weekly Sunday morning worship service, a Sunday night service, and a midweek prayer meeting. They didn't want the church to ever go "liberal."

Thirty years later, it took three years and a major rewrite of the constitution and bylaws to free up Sunday nights and Wednesday nights so that the church could launch a large-scale small group ministry.

That's ridiculous.

I know of another church whose constitution dictated that there be one elder for every one hundred members. That made sense in a church of four hundred. But at four thousand, it created a dysfunctional mess. Worse, short of a constitutional overhaul, the pastor had no way to get around it.

These examples illustrate why I've worked hard to keep our guiding documents as simple and flexible as possible. My ideal church constitution or bylaws would simply read, "We will honor God to the best of our ability."

While I know that's not legally possible and probably not even prudent, it's still far better than an overly restrictive, hyperdetailed, untrusting set of rules that effectively quench the Spirit and tie the hands of those whom God will raise up to lead this church in the future.

Rigid plans, guidelines, and regulations work fine in a stable environment. But if there is anything we know about the future, it's that it won't be anything like what we expected. The best thing today's leaders can do to serve future leaders is to give them the same freedom and flexibility that we want.

That's why it's important to plan in pencil. It makes tomorrow's midcourse corrections much easier to make.

Chapter 6

Clarifying the Pastor's Role

Why Leadership Matters

SO WHAT'S THE PROPER role of a pastor? Is it as the primary leader, taking charge and setting the agenda for ministry? Is it as a leader among equals? Is it as a church employee, carrying out the will of the board? Is it as the resident mystic, seeking God and sharing with everyone else a word from the Lord? Is it as a chaplain, fulfilling spiritual duties and functions while not getting too involved in the decision and direction-setting process?

Frankly, each of these roles can be appropriate. It all depends on the unique history, polity, size, personality, gifts, and calling that each pastor and local church bring to the equation.

But one thing is certain. Everyone needs to agree on the pastor's role. Otherwise, as we've already seen, it won't be long until dysfunction and conflict break out.

Another thing is equally certain. The role a pastor takes will determine to a great extent the church's potential for numerical growth. Pastors who don't lead, can't lead, or aren't allowed to lead seldom see their church break through growth barriers. It's as rare as a balmy day in the middle of a Chicago winter. It can happen, but it's bizarre when it does.

A Bad Day at the Pancake House

I'll never forget the day I realized that the board and I had radically different perceptions of my role. It was only a few weeks after I'd become the pastor of the small fledgling church that would eventually become North Coast Church.

The chairman of our elder board had been in Europe for an extended vacation when I candidated and was called to the church. While that seemed a little odd, everyone told me not to worry, that we'd get along great. They told me that as the former mayor of a large suburban city, he had a big vision for what God could do through our little church, and they assured me that he'd be a powerful force to help me fulfill God's vision and calling.

When the chairman returned from his trip, we arranged a meeting. As I pulled my old Toyota into the parking lot of the local pancake house, I was a bit nervous but mostly filled with excitement, enthusiasm, and lots of new ideas.

After the usual initial pleasantries, the chairman asked me what I had in mind for our ministry. For the next thirty minutes, I shared my dreams and vision while he ate and asked a few questions.

When I finished, he leaned across the table. "Son," he said, "don't you get too many fancy ideas. You just preach and pray. We'll run the church. And don't dig your roots too deep either, because it's a good idea for a pastor to move on every three or four years."

I was stunned.

During the entire interview process, my wife and I had talked about our commitment to long-term ministry, hopefully a lifetime ministry. Based on the responses of all those who interviewed us, we were sure that they wanted their pastor to have that kind of commitment as well as the ability to take the reins and set direction.

But that obviously wasn't the chairman's perspective. As far as he was concerned, I was an employee, not a leader. And something told me his opinions weren't to be taken lightly. Maybe it was the three hats he wore: board chairman, treasurer, and finance elder.

As I drove home, I knew the chairman and I had a serious problem. We each saw ourselves as occupying the same role, that of the initiating leader. And I knew from experience that you can't have two tigers on a hill.

At the time, I didn't realize how common my problems were. Role confusion is something that almost all pastors and leadership teams experience at one time or another. Even founding pastors have to deal with it. But it's particularly prevalent when there's been a significant turnover in lay leadership or when a new pastor comes to town. If the confusion is worked through quickly and healthily, it's no big deal. If it's left to fester, it can tear a ministry apart or lead to a full-on power struggle.

And that's what I feared most as I slowly navigated my way home.

Obviously, it's best if these issues are worked through at the beginning of a pastor's calling. But I've discovered that even then most boards, staffs, and congregations are far slower to let go of the reins than they claim. And few will really let go until three key questions have been answered to their satisfaction.

1. Is the pastor as committed to the church as I am? ·
2. Who is best qualified to lead, and why?
3. How can we prevent a strong leader from becoming a dictator?

Most people aren't even aware of these three questions, but they ask them just the same. Looking back, I realize that it wasn't until we'd satisfactorily worked our way through each one that I was granted the full freedom to lead.

1. Whose Church Is It?

The first thing that the people will want to know before they turn the reins over to a pastor is whether he is as committed to the church as they are. When a pastor finds, as I did, that some lay leaders and staff don't want to be led, it may be a matter of sinful pride. But more often it indicates that they see the pastor as an outsider. And no one who cares a lick about their church is going to hand it over to an outsider.

Obviously, the church doesn't belong to anyone. It's the Lord's. But there is a legitimate sense in which people speak of a local church as "their church." Anyone who has poured significant time, money, and energy into a congregation rightfully feels some sense of protective ownership.

A new pastor usually has an easy time leading these people — as long as it's on the exact same road they've already been traveling.

But try suggesting a significant change in direction and the question, "Whose church is this?" pops up front and center.

It starts with phone calls and emails asking, "What is *he* trying to do to *our* church?" Those pronouns are important. Listen for them. Until everyone is convinced that the pastor is as committed to the church's long-term health as they are, they'll tend to resist strong leadership, especially when it threatens to take them in a new direction.

To overcome this resistance, a pastor needs two things: time and personal commitment. We can't do much about the passage of time. And exactly how much time is needed depends on a variety of factors, such as the age of the church, the length of the previous pastorate, and the pastor's age in relation to the others on the leadership team.

But demonstrating long-term commitment to the church is a different matter. It can be done, but it starts with an honest look inside. I always ask pastors to honestly answer this question before attempting to take a strong leadership role: *is this a step in my career path, or is this a long-term calling to these people and this community?*

It doesn't have to be a lifetime calling to be a long-term calling. But five to seven years is far more a career step than a commitment. And if it's a temporary gig, there's no use pretending that it's *your* church too. It'd be better to take on the role of a consultant and caring outsider.

Committed for the Long Haul

Even if the founding pastor or a new pastor believes that God has called him to have a long-term commitment, that doesn't mean much if nobody believes it.

And many won't, for good reason.

Their past experiences tell them not to.

Our board chairman, for example, had seen many a pastor come and go during his years. And since our church was small and struggling, and I was young and "on my way up," he was sure I would be gone as soon as a better opportunity presented itself. No wonder he was hesitant to turn over the reins.

Let's be honest. When a tough crisis comes along, many pastors bail out. One denominational study found that a pastoral crisis occurs every eighteen months. Coincidentally, pastors from this same group moved on an average of every eighteen to twenty months. Something tells me there might be a connection.

While these pastors spoke of a calling, their résumés revealed something that looked far more like a career track. And when things dried up, most of them went searching for greener pastures.

It's no wonder that boards, staffs, and congregations often respond with a kneejerk "No" when a new pastor suggests anything risky. They're trying to protect their church from a mess they're pretty sure the new guy won't stay around to help clean up.

In my case, our board members and congregation had to see me demonstrate my long-term commitment with my finances, my use of time, and a couple of decisions to stay even when more enticing opportunities and bigger platforms came my way. They had to be convinced that I was more concerned about *our church* than *my ministry*. Once that happened, it was amazing how open they were to being led.

What If You Can't Stay, or Don't Want to Stay?

Obviously, many pastors can't stay for the long haul due to personal, geographical, or even denominational constraints. That's okay, as long as we don't usurp the authority and leadership of those who will be there for the long run.

If, for whatever reason, a pastor knows his stay will be short, it's far better to take the role of an influential consultant than to take the role of a strong directional leader. The only exceptions would be when a dying church is on life support or when a church in crisis is about to crash and burn. In those situations, someone has to take charge before the whole church collapses.

As an example of an influential consultant role, take my friend Aaron. He served in a denomination that moved him to a new parish every three to five years. He saw no reason to battle for the reins; he knew he would lose. So when he arrived at a new church, he quickly figured out who the real power brokers were. Then he poured his life into theirs. He knew that long after he was gone, they'd still be running the show. He chose influence rather than directional leadership, preferring to leave his fingerprints rather than his stamp on everything he touched. As a result, the churches he served benefited greatly from his wisdom.

The bottom line is that a pastor who wants to take on the privilege of strong leadership has to give up the freedom of loose commitment.

2. Who Is Best Qualified to Lead?

The second thing that people need to know before they allow a pastor to lead is whether he's the one best qualified to lead. Until most people think so, it will be hard for him to lead.

So what makes a pastor most qualified? Why not the chairman of the board, another layperson, or the entire board or staff working together?

The answer is simple. In most cases, the pastor is best qualified to lead not because of superior spirituality, intelligence, or even leadership skills but because of two key factors: time and training.

Time

As a full-time pastor, I'm immersed in the day-to-day ministry of our church. Unlike any of my board members (and most staff members), I'm thinking about the big picture of our ministry all the time. By virtue of my full-time role, I have the time to analyze our problems, scope out our opportunities, seek wise counsel, meet with people, and study what others are doing to a degree that would be impossible for the others on our leadership team.

Wise leadership demands an understanding of the whole, how all the parts fit together, and how each one will be affected by any proposed changes. That takes time, lots of it. This kind of leadership can't be done on a part-time basis except in the smallest of churches. In a church with a multiple staff, it takes at least fifty to sixty hours a week.

It's not that lay leaders are incapable of leading an organization. That's what many of them do for a living. But they lead their organizations on a full-time basis. None of them would think of trying to do it in his or her spare time. Yet that is exactly what happens when a board or powerful lay leader tries to take on the directional leadership role in the church. They try to do something they'd never do in their own business. It's no surprise that it never works.

Training

The pastor also has a decided advantage when it comes to training. Most pastors have participated in formal education and ongoing studies designed specifically to equip them to lead a church. Add to that their network of fellow pastors and church leaders, and they have a wealth of information from which to draw.

When the church faces a tough situation or a golden opportunity, the pastor is usually the one most likely to have been exposed to a similar situation. If he hasn't, he'll usually know someone who's gone through it or what the experts recommend.

By contrast, most board members and lay leaders are limited in their exposure to other ministries. They don't have the time to read the literature. Their network of ministry experts is usually limited to a previous pastor or two. And because the church is spiritually centered, volunteer-run, and educationally focused, it's very different from the organizations they may have experience in leading.

Are there exceptions? Certainly, but that's the point: they're *exceptions*. I know of one great church in the Midwest where a successful businessman has been the unquestioned directional leader. It has worked incredibly well, but that's because of his off-the-charts leadership gifts and the agreement of everyone on the team that he's the best qualified to be in charge.

More common though is the experience of a friend of mine whose board (with his full support) tried to follow an "elder-led" model that called on him to focus on prayer, teaching, and counseling while they ran the church. When he told me what they were planning to do and why it was so biblical, I told him it wouldn't work.

I don't think he appreciated my candor or my theology — at least not at first.

His team was idealistically convinced that they could run an entire church (and make fully informed, wise decisions) on just a few meetings a month as long as they picked the right people and trained them properly, thus freeing up their pastor to "seek God."

What my friend and his board failed to notice was that the New Testament churches they were trying to model themselves after were small, meeting mostly in homes, while his church was pushing four hundred in weekend attendance.

He also liked to point out that the apostles turned the administration of the church over to deacons while they focused on prayer and the Word. But last I looked, it was only the apostles who gave themselves to full-time prayer and ministry of the Word, not necessarily every church leader and pastor.

My friend and his team also failed to notice that the church they had learned this from and were modeling themselves after was filled with self-employed and independently wealthy lay leaders who had all the time in the world to give to the church. And on top of that, they were located near a top-notch seminary that provided them with professors and other experienced ministry types to help lead the church.

My friend's elders, on the other hand, all had jobs that called for forty to fifty hours a week plus a long commute. They didn't have the time, training, or inclination to take a strong leadership role. So the church floundered.

Not surprisingly, my friend was "called" to another ministry a few years later, where he decided it might be a good idea if someone was in charge.

What If the Pastor Is Not Cut Out for a Strong Leadership Role?

Sometimes a pastor may not be cut out for strong leadership. That's no big deal in a smaller church that is willing to stay small or in a larger church where another staff member or key lay leader is capable of picking up the slack.

For instance, I know of one church where the associate pastor was a far stronger leader than the senior pastor, so the pastor let him lead. They had known each other a long time, and they had a great deal of mutual trust and respect, so it worked well for them.

Yet, while this type of arrangement is far better than stalling out or going nowhere, it can have some unintended negative consequences. Perhaps the biggest is that it can create a huge problem for the next pastor, particularly if he's a gifted leader and wants to take back the reins.

But one thing will never work: the pastor can't be a Jekyll-and-Hyde leader, someone who abdicates leadership and then jumps in to micromanage. That guarantees confusion, frustration, and often some rather creative forms of passive aggression.

3. Can a Strong Leader Be Controlled?

The third thing people want to know before letting a leader lead is that strong leadership won't become a dictatorship. Everyone fears a dictator, even a benevolent one. Anything that smacks of domineering leadership will be resisted. Nearly every longtime Christian, board member, or staff member has a horror story of a strong leader gone bad.

This is a particularly big fear in churches like mine that have a heritage of congregational government. To some of these folks, strong leadership and dictatorship are synonymous. Before they'll let a pastor lead, they have to be thoroughly convinced that appropriate checks and balances are firmly in place.

Personally, I'm good with that. I know my sin nature too well. That's why I've committed myself to follow three key guidelines.

1. Present first drafts, not final proposals
2. Keep no secrets from the board
3. Follow the board's advice

These guidelines ensure that my leadership has boundaries and help keep me accountable. They also go a long way toward allaying the fears of those who are suspicious of strong leadership.

1. Present First Drafts, Not Final Proposals

I always present first drafts, not final proposals. By this, I don't mean that I offer half-baked ideas or suggestions off the top of my head. My first drafts are carefully thought out and persuasively presented. But I don't confuse them with God's final revealed will. That's something the board, staff, and I will determine together.

A strong, initiating leader who presents everything in final form puts the rest of the team in an awkward position. Those that hate conflict become rubber stamps. Those that fear domination dig in and become adversarial, either aggressively or passive-aggressively.

I have a friend who is very bright and gifted. He takes his position as a spiritual leader seriously. He often prays and fasts over major decisions and initiatives. But one thing he seldom does is consult anyone else in the process. His ideas come out fully hatched. They are presented to his staff and board as being straight from the Lord, often accompanied by, "This is what God is showing me."

Now, who can argue with that?

Not many on his staff can. Not many on his board do.

But a couple of board members who fear the idea of pastoral domination drive him nuts because they resist almost everything he presents. Even when they might have agreed with his proposal, the more strongly he presents it, the more they put up a fight. It's the only way they know to keep from being run over.

He writes them off as carnal.

I've told him they're not carnal; they're frightened.

By presenting first drafts rather than a take-it-or-leave-it finished proposal, I send a message to my staff and our board that I'm open to changes in my plan. Once people realize that your ideas can be altered, they'll quit resisting the plan as a whole and start pointing out their areas of concern.

Who knows, their concerns might be legitimate.

I've often found that they are.

2. Keep No Secrets from the Board

My second guideline is to keep no secrets from the board. I've discovered that keeping anything from the board puts them at a decided disadvantage and sets me up as being unaccountable.

If I know something of a sensitive nature and keep it from them, the board will inevitably make a different decision than they would have if they'd had all the facts. Or worse, I'll have to pull the "trust me, I know something I can't tell you" card. Either way, keeping secrets from the board is a losing proposition.

I didn't always feel this way. I used to see no reason why the board needed to know anything about the spiritual and moral struggles that people went through. That was privileged communication between pastor and parishioner. But when it came to making decisions about people, the board and I had two sets of information, and that tended to lead to opposite conclusions and some awkward dilemmas.

To put an end to this predicament, I started telling everyone who asked for strict confidentiality that I couldn't promise it. If they told me something that the elders needed to know about or that I needed help in figuring out, I didn't want to be backed into a confidentiality corner.

To my surprise, few people ever objected. No one has ever gotten upset or angry. No one has ever left the church over it. They know that nothing will be shared unless I deem it absolutely necessary, and they know the character of our elders and senior pastors.

I ask those who do object to go elsewhere with the information, on the premise that it is better not to know something important than to know it, need to share it, and be unable to do so.

Of course, I share this kind of information only when absolutely necessary. But my refusal to promise confidentiality allows me to share information the board needs to know in order to make wise decisions. And that's important because we have a joint responsibility to shepherd and lead the flock, and we can't do our job if we keep secrets from one another.

I've also learned that it's important to keep the board in the loop about what's happening with our staff. It's a lesson I learned the hard way.

My first hire didn't work out so well. During his first year, I received numerous complaints about his failure to follow through. But I kept these comments to myself, figuring that it was my role to be a staff advocate.

It didn't take long for some board members to hear the same things. That led one of our elders at a year-end budget meeting to suggest letting him go. During the discussion, I made no mention of the complaints I'd received or my own growing frustration. I assumed it was my job to defend the staff. I pointed out all the good things he had done. They ended up giving him a small raise.

Later, when I realized things weren't going to work out (along with the procrastination problems, he was now badmouthing me to others), I went to the board and told them we needed to make a change.

They were dumfounded. How could I defend his work one day and months later ask for his release?

When I explained what had really been going on, and thus what I'd kept from them, a couple of elders became indignant. Why hadn't they been informed of this before?

The sad truth was that I hadn't trusted them to deal with the information. I was afraid they might overreact. But my decision to keep important facts to myself only revealed the hollowness of my claims to believe in accountability and teamwork. I had arrogantly manipulated our board by keeping them in the dark because of my prideful belief that only I could handle the truth.

It was a big mistake. It was wrong. I vowed that it would never happen again. And it hasn't.

3. Follow the Board's Advice

My third guideline is to follow the board's advice. This ensures that my strong leadership has boundaries. I've found that strong and gifted leaders often confuse leadership with infallibility. They assume that submitting to others means abdicating their leadership role. Nothing could be farther from the truth.

I've committed myself to listen to and follow the board's advice for two reasons. It's the best way to undercut fears of domination. And more important, it's the best way to become a wiser leader.

Wisdom is found in heeding counsel, even (or especially) when I think the advice is wrong. The fact is, I can be right about *what* we're supposed to do but dead wrong about *when* we're supposed to do it. Over the years, God has often used the resistance of others to polish a good idea and turn it into a great idea. Sometimes he's also used that resistance to expose a brain cramp that I thought was a flash of inspiration.

There are only two circumstances under which I would not submit to the board's direction: (1) if they wanted me to violate what I understood to be the clear, black-and-white teaching of Scripture; (2) if they asked me to disobey what I understood to be the clear and unmistakable voice of the Lord.

I've never been asked to violate Scripture, and only once have I ever faced resistance to something I was *absolutely sure* that God had told me.

It happened when I was pushing for us to hire someone in our church to be my first full-time staff member (not the guy I fired). While he was a gifted and anointed man of God, at that time he lacked a seminary education and had never worked in a church. Understandably, some of the board members were hesitant; they wanted to hire someone who had been around the block before.

They turned me down. But that night while I was driving home, it was as if I heard the literal voice of God say, "Hire Mike."

I knew it wasn't last night's pizza. It was God. I knew it beyond a shadow of a doubt. So I went back to the board and told them, "I know it sounds strange, but God told me on the way home that we're supposed to hire Mike."

Some board members were taken aback. A couple pushed back.

But eventually they all agreed to give Mike a shot. They knew that I don't throw around the "God told me" card lightly. In fact, it was the first time they'd ever heard me use it in regard to a decision we were making, and for some, it was the first time they'd heard me use it period. So they gave me the benefit of the doubt.

It turned out to be one of the most important decisions we ever made. Within months, even those who had been most vocal in their opposition were singing Mike's praises.

Here's the key point: if I hadn't previously submitted to their decisions that I didn't agree with, there's no way they would have listened to me when I played the "God told me" card. It would have been seen as just another creative ploy to get my own way.

Research has consistently shown that strong pastoral leadership is a key ingredient in virtually every healthy and growing church. But this leadership can't be demanded or taken. It has to be granted. To be given freedom to lead, a pastor first has to help people answer the three lingering questions that every board, congregation, and staff member asks. Once these questions are answered, a pastor will not have a hard time taking the reins. Most people actually want to be led. They just don't want to be led by a hired mercenary who's unqualified and who just might use his leadership position to take advantage of those he leads.

It reminds me of something Jesus said about leadership: "Whoever wants to become great among you must be your servant, and whoever wants to be first must be your slave — just as the Son of Man did not come to be served, but to serve, and to give his life as a ransom for many."[10]

Chapter 7

Clarifying Board and Staff Roles

Why Teamwork Matters

HEALTHY TEAMS HAVE GREAT teamwork. There's little role confusion, and everyone knows what the ultimate goal is. More important, successful teams set aside personal agendas and preferences to get the bigger job done.

Contrast that with sick and dysfunctional teams. They have none of these traits. Instead, they're riddled with an abundance of role confusion, lots of drama, and various goals and agendas vying for priority.

If you've ever been on a board or staff like that, you know how disheartening it can be. And if you've ever tried to lead a splintered and dysfunctional team (if you can call it a team), you know that it can make bailing out of the ministry seem like a tempting option.

That's why it's so important to address role confusion and competing agendas before they break out. There's not much a leader can do once things fall apart. It's hard to put Humpty Dumpty back together again. In most cases, it takes years and a major turnover of teammates before things can get back on track.

One of the best ways to cut off disharmony and dysfunction at the pass is to clarify board roles and staff roles before someone joins the team — *and to make sure that everyone knows that changes in these roles will be unavoidable and necessary as the church grows.*

Much like the changes in relationship and communication patterns that take place when a team goes from playing golf to football, changes in the primary role of the board and the staff are unavoidable. But they aren't always welcomed or understood.

That's why addressing them ahead of time is so important. It's the best way to minimize the whitewater. Let's face it, many of the harshest conflicts in church leadership teams can be traced to differing role expectations, and sometimes to just one board or staff member who refuses to accept a role they don't like and makes a stink about it.

The Changing Roles of the Board

The primary role of the board will always be the same: to determine God's will and then see that it's carried out. But the process of how this is best done and what role the board should take will change as the church changes.

Doing

In a small church, ministry is an all-hands-on-deck affair. There is always far more work to be done than people to do it. At this stage, most board members (if the church even has a board) have a clearly defined frontline ministry role and are involved in *doing* practically everything.

When I first arrived at North Coast, one elder handled the finances, another handled worship, and still another oversaw our children's ministry. I was grateful for all the help I could get. I certainly couldn't do everything myself, and these areas of ministry were all small enough to be handled on a part-time basis.

But as the church grew, some of these ministries needed more time and focus than any of our elders could offer. So we hired some part-time staff members, and our board suddenly needed to redefine its role from being the de facto staff to being more like a true leadership board.

Approving

As our church began to grow, the board members moved from the role of *doing* practically everything to *approving* almost everything. Not that they stopped serving in hands-on areas of ministry, but they now spent most of their time reviewing options and making decisions on anything of substance, from debating the purchase of a new computer, to altering the order of the worship service, to approving a new Sunday school teacher or nursery worker.

The role of approving fits perfectly a small to midsize church. We were still small enough that board members had a solid grasp of what was happening and how their decisions would impact the entire church. Because our budget was tight, it was also prudent to have a group carefully examining and approving expenditures ahead of time.

Unfortunately, some board members try to hold on to this role long after it's appropriate or effective. I often hear from pastors in churches that are large enough to have multiple services and multiple staff members that the entire leadership team has been sidetracked or held hostage by a single board member who insists on operating in the approval zone.

This is always a clear sign of either major trust issues or a board that doesn't understand that growth changes everything, including the role they should play. And if no one has the insight or guts to say, "Stop it!" then frustration, infighting, and conflict are sure to increase.

Reviewing

With our continued growth, the process of always seeking approval ahead of time eventually started to bog things down. Our meetings began to drag on later and later, often far into the night. Even worse, the board's decisions no longer fit the unique circumstances of our ministry as much as they reflected what worked or didn't work at their place of employment.

The increased size and complexity of our ministry left most of them out of touch with much of what was happening on the front lines. They had little understanding of how their decisions actually impacted the volunteers and staff. So they defaulted to the world they knew best: their own workplace.

It was time to change the board's role again; this time from *approving* almost everything ahead of time to *reviewing* most things after the fact.

Our agenda changed. We no longer debated which copier to buy; instead, we set a budget and let the people who would use the copier decide which one they wanted and which features they needed most. Major decisions still needed approval, but many of the items we'd previously discussed at length became simple bullet points and FYIs.

As with each stage, this change in their role met some resistance. Most of it came from a couple of board members who feared losing control and had a strong bent toward risk aversion. But it wasn't that hard to win them over once they realized that the staff couldn't do too much damage in the thirty days between meetings. And if things did get off track, the board still retained the right to pull back the leash and redefine the kind of things that needed prior approval.

The promise of getting everyone home before midnight helped a lot too.

Setting Direction and Boundaries

As the church continued to grow, the review process became terminally boring. Each month, we suffered through a bunch of tedious and dull reports that, frankly, were full of fluff. No one paid attention (well, except the one guy whose questions irritated the rest of us because they prolonged an already too long meeting). It was obviously time for the board to change roles again.

At this point, the increasing complexity of our ministry called for something much closer to a board governance model. The board needed to shift from *reviewing* almost everything to *setting direction and boundaries*. At North Coast, this involves setting North Star goals and operational boundaries. The board then steps back and lets the paid staff figure out how to accomplish these goals.

Some things are still worthy of review (budgets, benchmarks, and evaluations, for example). And some things still need approval (major initiatives, most staff hires, and anything else that could have a significant impact on the ministry). In addition, we have a "no surprises" rule to assure the board that they are being kept in the loop.

But at this stage, the board has to give up all forms of micro-management and preference management ("I would have done it that way").

Now, that's not easy to do. It's human nature to kibitz, especially when we have the advantage of twenty-twenty hindsight. But when a board takes on the role of setting direction and boundaries, it has to release micromanagement and preference management. Other-wise, the ministry staff will quickly grow gun-shy and sometimes even revert back to seeking approval for everything so as to not be second-guessed. And if that happens, it won't be long until your meetings start pushing midnight again and most of your gifted staff members start sending out résumés.

In a large church, if the board can't trust the pastor and staff to make good operational decisions, tighter control is seldom the best solution. More likely, it's time for a new pastor and staff. But if the pastor and staff can be trusted, the board needs to step back and let them do what they've been hired to do, without nitpicking the process or details.

Frankly, this final transition can be particularly tough for board members who successfully manage their own staff or who own a business. They are often so used to being the unquestioned boss that they can't let go of critiquing the details. They tend to forget that the church staff is not their staff and the church is not their business.

One sure sign that someone is having a hard time letting go is a sudden uptick in complaints about not being "listened to." While that might indeed be the case, I've found that "You don't listen" often means "You didn't do what I suggested." And if that's the case, it's usually time for a little role clarification.

When Should Changes in the Board's Role Be Made?

The strongest indicators that it's time to consider changing the primary role of the board are (1) a marked increase in conflict and frustration while making decisions and (2) meetings that drag on forever.

I'm often asked at what attendance size or staff size these changes in the board's role should be made. Unfortunately, there are no universal benchmarks. Most often, the need for these changes is experienced more as a sliding scale than a tectonic shift. Each situation is unique. Though the stages and transitions are sequential and predictable, each church goes through them at a different pace.

If they go through them, that is.

Some boards steadfastly resist any changes in their role. They'd rather cap their growth and turn over pastors and staff at a steady clip than lose their tight control. Obviously, these are the boards that most need this book, but alas, they are the least likely to ever read it.

What If Your Church Goes Mega?

Obviously, most churches will never become a so-called megachurch. But those that do can expect even greater challenges, especially if the church has a long history under a previous pastor or if most of the current growth followed a long period of no growth or slow growth.

Overnight megachurches (I call them "Baby Huey churches") have their own issues, but one thing they don't have to deal with is a lot of baggage from the past. No one squawks about messing with traditions or "the way we've always done things around here"; they don't have a past to remember and idealize.

North Coast didn't hit mega status overnight. It took over a decade. And when we got there, I was surprised at how out of touch our board had become with the day-to-day aspects of our ministry — not just out of touch but completely out of touch.

We now have multiple services on multiple days at multiple campuses, and it is no longer possible for board members to wrap their arms around our ministry. Even those of us who work at it full-time have a hard time knowing what is going on.

I knew we were in a new world when someone we were seriously considering as a nominee for our elder board was unknown to four of our current elders and one of our senior staff members. They had never heard of or seen the person before.

At that point, it was obvious that we needed to redefine the role of our elder board in ways I'd not foreseen.

First, we had to redefine our *spiritual role*. There were simply too many people for us to know or spiritually care for. We had to find a way to push our role as spiritual shepherds out to the front lines. In our case, that meant making sure that our small groups offered the same kind of spiritual oversight and care that we'd always seen ourselves as responsible for.

In essence, we began to function more like the leaders of a mini-denomination than of a typical local church. We retained global spiritual oversight, but the hands-on work of praying for our people, caring for their needs, and nurturing the flock largely had to be turned over to others. We became ranchers overseeing shepherds.

Second, we had to redefine the board's *primary governance role*. While the board still continued to set North Star direction and ministry boundaries, at times they wondered what they were there for. Since they no longer approved every decision or reviewed every action, and since the church now had a staff that ran things well, at the end of some meetings the board was left wondering, "What are we here for?"

To help clarify the board's role in an increasingly staff-led church, we identified the following three key functions (along with setting direction and boundaries).

1. *Wise counsel.* The larger our staff-led church gets, the more I need advice from those who are outside the day-to-day grind. If the staff makes up our royal court, the board makes up our council of wise sages and advisors. They offer a perspective that those of us deeply immersed in the day-to-day ministry can easily miss.

2. *Brakes.* Our board holds the keys to accountability. Should anything go amiss with me or the staff, the board is the one group that can immediately slam on the brakes. While they don't micromanage our expenses or programming decisions (we usually spend five to ten minutes max talking about our budget unless something is out of whack), they have the right to stop anything, anytime, if needed.

3. *A crisis team in waiting.* When a genuine crisis hits, it's too late to try to throw together a team of godly and wise folks who have enough history and understanding of each other to work through the tough calls, sharp disagreements, and dicey issues that come with any major mess. If these people aren't already in place, it's hard to throw them together on the fly and even harder to navigate your way through the landmines. Our board provides the security of knowing we have such a team already in place. Like firefighters playing cards in the firehouse, they're prepared, connected, and ready if the bell should ring — and some days, bored enough to wish it would ring.

The Changing Roles of the Staff

Board members aren't the only ones who have to work through significant role changes as the church grows; so do pastors and staff members. And as with board members, if staff members don't make these adjustments, the ministry will quickly become a battleground of personal agendas and stalled-out growth.

Often the toughest transitions happen when growth forces the changes in relational patterns that we already looked at in "What Game Are We Playing?" (chapter 4). But there are also other role changes that staff members must make as the church grows.

From Generalist to Specialist

In a smaller church, staff members tend to be generalists. They are more likely to be good at many things than world-class at any one thing. They almost certainly wear more than one hat. They almost always have a high degree of hands-on responsibility as opposed to oversight responsibilities.

But as the church grows, the need for specialized skills emerges. It's a natural by-product of the growing complexity that comes with increased attendance and programs.

Unfortunately, switching from being a *generalist* to a *specialist* is a difficult change. It can leave a generalist feeling lost and confused, not to mention inadequate. For instance, a generalist who can build up the junior high program to fifteen kids, while also overseeing the elementary Sunday school ministry, often doesn't have the skill set to grow it to forty. But that's the expectation in a church that is large enough to hire multiple specialists.

Frankly, when a church hits this stage, there's not much a generalist can do except find something to excel at or find another small church in need of a generalist.

I know that's harsh. But it's true.

This is often a terribly painful transition for both the generalist and the lead pastor. The pastor feels angst over the idea of pushing out someone who has done nothing wrong. And the generalist often feels betrayed by an organization that has outgrown his or her capacity to serve. It's a tough place to be when a formerly prized skill is no longer needed or affirmed.

That's not to say there isn't room for a few generalists in a larger church. But the generalists who succeed are usually high-capacity generalists who can do many things at the same level as a specialist.

From Doing to Empowering

As a church grows larger still, staff members who are specialists need to move from *doing* everything themselves to *empowering* others.

This too is not always an easy transition. Many specialists love hands-on control. They have a hard time finding others who can do what they do to their satisfaction. After all, they are specialists.

But if these folks don't switch to an empowering model rather than a do-it-myself model, everything will eventually come to a screeching halt.

For instance, let's take the case of a worship pastor. In most cases, a full-time worship pastor is hired to actually lead worship. It's a *doing* role. But eventually, a worship pastor who sees his or her role as primarily leading worship puts a lid on growth. Additional worship services or venue options will be limited by the worship pastor's physical capacity to be present or by the church's financial ability to keep hiring additional worship leaders.

In contrast, an empowerment model removes the lid. It doesn't ask the specialist to do everything; it asks the specialist to find, develop, and empower others to do everything.

At North Coast Church, our worship pastor has long been paid to raise up other worship leaders. I don't want an all-star band. I want a stable of quality musicians and worship leaders. I don't want an incredible musician who caps our ministry. I want an empowering musician who leverages our ministry.

Because of this, we've always been able to add services quickly and cheaply when needed. We aren't limited by the physical capacity of our worship leader to be present or by our budget's ability to hire additional worship leaders.

As I write this, we have over twenty adult worship bands. Even before we added all the venues and worship options that we currently have, we had four full bands that rotated through our worship service each month. So when the time came to expand our worship options, they were ready and eager to help us do so.

The same thing holds true in almost every area of ministry, from youth pastors to administrators, from office support staff to children's workers. Specialists who can't become trainers or who aren't willing to become trainers will eventually put a ceiling on the growth of your church or bust your budget.

This transition can be especially difficult for perfectionists. By their nature and personality, they can never find anyone who measures up to their ability to do it themselves. It can also be difficult for up-front performers (teachers, worship leaders, and those involved in the arts). They often don't want to share the limelight.

Both perfectionists and performers may resist empowering others. But don't let them. If you do, they'll sabotage your ability to reach more people for Christ.

My Silo to Our Church

Another change that staff members must adjust to as the church grows is a transition from focusing primarily on their own ministry area to asking, "What's best for the church as a whole?"

In most situations, the success of a youth, children's, or worship ministry contributes to the success of the entire church. But eventually most growing churches end up with a complex matrix of specialized ministries that start to compete internally for resources and attention. It's at this point that turf battles, volunteer raids, and budget wars often break out. The solution is a change in perspective. Staff members have to stop asking, "What is best for my ministry?" and start asking, "What is best for the church as a whole?"

I see a larger church as being a lot like the USA Olympic basketball team. Every player on the squad is a superstar in his own right. But at the Olympic level, some of those players have to sublimate their individual skills and potential for the good of the team. They have to intentionally take on a role that is less than their best.

It's the same in a church with lots of competing ministries. Some of them have to be willing to be less than their best for the good of the whole.

For instance, at North Coast Church, our small groups are the hub of our ministry and the primary vehicle for relationships, discipleship, and church health. For over twenty-five years, we've had more than 80 percent of our weekend attendance involved in these sermon-based (think lecture-lab) study groups.[11] To reach and maintain that high percentage, we have to cut the competition. We have to ask some of our other ministries to scale back.

That's why our children's ministry is not allowed to have a midweek program, no matter how great it might be for the kids and their ministry. We've found that most people will only give us two time slots per week (including the weekend worship service). If we had a midweek children's program, the volunteer staffing needs would cut into our ability to get parents into small groups. And for the sake of the entire ministry, we believe a growing mom and dad is far more important than an awesome children's program.

We take the same approach with North Coast U, a ministry that offers deeper study in everything from theology to life skills. I have no doubt that North Coast U could be huge, offering ministry not only to our church but to our entire region. But once again, allowing North Coast U to reach its full potential would undercut the most important thing we do. So we hamstring it, making sure that all of its workshops and courses start *after* people have already signed up and started their small group sessions and offering most of the courses during the summer, when our small groups don't meet.

This can be hard for high-drive staff members to accept, especially those who judge their competence and worth in light of the success and growth of their silo. But it has to be done — or they have to move on.

It takes a special kind of staff member (an ultimate team player) to be willing to do their best when their best is intentionally hamstrung. But that's the kind of staff member a larger church needs, especially once the matrix of ministries becomes large enough to compete for limited resources and time.

A ministry can't remain healthy and vibrant when behind-the-scenes turf battles, budget wars, and volunteer raids are taking place. Fiefdoms and silos might make for strong programming, but the price is a sick church.

Chapter 8

Making Room at the Top

Why Young Eagles Don't Stay

IN HIGH SCHOOL, I noticed a strange phenomenon. The freshmen got smaller every year. It was really weird.

When my friends and I walked onto campus for the first day of our freshman year, we were legit high schoolers, admittedly a little intimidated by the seniors but plenty cool in our own right.

Not so with the punks that came in the next year. Something must have happened at the middle school to stunt their growth. None of the new ninth graders were anywhere near as big, smart, or mature as we had been the year before. And by the time I was a senior, the middle school was pumping out mental, physical, and emotional midgets.

As I said, it was really strange.

Of course, that's not what was happening. The freshmen weren't getting smaller, stupider, and less mature; we were getting older, more mature, and arrogant.

Fortunately for each incoming crop of freshmen, the seniors keep graduating, giving last year's freshmen, sophomores, and juniors an opportunity to spread their wings and fly. And sure enough, they always ended up flying a lot higher than the seniors would have guessed.

In the church, it's a different story. The seniors never graduate (at least not until they've become literal seniors and start dying off). They hog the leadership table, shutting out the next generation. It's one of the main reasons that most churches stop growing and lose their evangelistic touch (and cultural relevance) around the twenty-year mark.

Letting Young Eagles Fly

Ironically, most churches are started by young eagles. But soon after getting their nest built, nicely appointed, and fully furnished, they start to marginalize the next batch of young eagles, asking them to sit at the kids' table and wait for their turn at middle-aged leadership.

To counteract that natural tendency, I've made it a personal priority to make sure that our young eagles have a place at our leadership table. I see it as my role to enhance their influence within our church, making sure that they are supported, protected, and listened to.

But I have to admit, it's not always appreciated, especially by middle-aged eagles who think that tenure should be the primary determiner of influence.

I understand their reluctance. Young eagles can make a mess in the cage. They're impatient. They lack the wisdom that comes with experience. In short, they make the same dumb mistakes that the old eagles made when they first started out.

But that's not the real reason that most churches and leadership teams push young eagles out of the nest. The real reason is that leadership is a zero-sum game. One person's emerging influence is always another person's waning influence. That's why making room for the young eagles is a hard sell, especially to those who already have a place at the table.

Again, I understand. Like most leaders, I love the *idea* of servant leadership and putting others first, as long as no one actually cuts in front of me or starts treating me like I'm a servant.

But it has to be done or we'll fall victim to the predictable twenty-year death cycle that causes most churches to stop growing, evangelizing, and making a mark.

When a church grows old, gray, and culturally out of touch — far more interested in protecting the past than in creating the future — it starts to wonder, "What happened to all the young people that used to hang around here?" That's a sure sign that the young eagles have been shut out for a long time.

I'd be a liar if I said that protecting and promoting young eagles is a pain-free venture. It's far easier in theory than in practice. I don't like giving up my personal power, prestige, or preferences any more than the next guy does. It's kind of a drag.

But young eagles are born to fly. It's their nature. It's how God made them. If they can't fly high in our church, they'll bolt and fly elsewhere. And sadly, if and when they do, they'll take most of the life, vitality, and the future of the church with them.

So, honestly now, how are you and your church responding to young eagles? Are they written off, tolerated, or celebrated? Are they encouraged to fly or asked to clip their wings?

I guarantee you, your answer will determine your church's future.

When working with leadership teams to determine their ability and openness to fully utilize and keep young eagles, I ask three questions.

1. Are young eagles empowered *and* platformed?
2. Are young eagles in the loop or in the meeting?
3. Who gets to ride shotgun?

Once I know the answers to these three questions, it's relatively easy to predict with great accuracy whether young eagles are flying high or flying away.

I must warn you, however. If you are over fifty, already have a seat at the leadership table, and perhaps think most of the new eagles you know are a lot like the shrinking freshmen I encountered in high school, you might not like what you read next.

1. Are Young Eagles Empowered *and* Platformed?

I find that most ministries pride themselves on *empowering* people. But I seldom hear anyone talk about *platforming* people. Yet empowerment without a platform is like responsibility without authority. It's frustrating for everyone involved.

Platforming is granting someone the symbols of power and prestige. It tells everyone that this person has significant juice, influence, and power.

These symbols of power and prestige vary from one organization and industry to another. But everyone within knows exactly what they mean. In the business world, it's the corner office, a private parking space, or an impressive title on your business card. In an academic setting, it's the letters after your name or the title "professor" rather than "instructor" (even if you're teaching exactly the same material). In a church, it's the title you're given, the role you're allowed to play, and a host of other subtle symbols.

I grew up in a church where it was pretty clear to all of us that the senior pastor was the only real pastor. Though there were two others on staff, he always carried out the symbolic duties of spiritual authority: communion, baptisms, weddings, and burials.

That sent a strong message to every other eagle (young and old) that if you wanted to fly in the pastoral world, you'd better go elsewhere. His was a platform not to be shared.

The senior pastor's hogging of the symbols and platforms of spiritual leadership also sent a strong message to the congregation. If someone was in the hospital, he had to be the one to visit. His were the only prayers that counted. If someone needed spiritual counsel, or even the keys to the church kitchen, he was always the one you called.

The result was an overwhelmed pastor and two devalued associates.

But it doesn't have to be that way. Leaders who willingly share the symbols of organizational power experience a completely different reality. Since their young eagles (and any other eagles they have on the team) don't have to go elsewhere to fly, they tend to stay.

When a congregation has other gifted, powerful, and appropriately platformed leaders to choose from, people will start turning to them for spiritual counsel and the keys to the kitchen, significantly lightening the pastoral load.

We can platform people in many ways. Most involve simply stepping back and sharing some of the platforms and perks you already have. The following are some of the most effective strategies I've used over the years. They have helped our young eagles (and other eagles on our team) fly higher and stay longer. I don't offer them as a prescription. They're examples. I realize that each ministry is unique. What works in one setting can easily bomb in another. So you'll have to figure out what will work in your unique ministry environment.

Titles

Years ago, I had a great associate pastor that I didn't want to lose. He shared the pulpit with me and was an integral part of what God was doing in our church. Yet people were constantly asking him when he was going to get his own church. They weren't hoping he would go; they were worried he would leave. But the question itself was a devaluing question. It sent a message that staying here was somehow a sign of failure, while going elsewhere was a promotion.

Now, there is nothing wrong with the title "associate pastor." But in my faith tradition, it has come to mean that you either are too young to be a senior pastor or lack the gifts to be a senior pastor. So people assume that anyone who has strong preaching and leadership gifts (and the title "associate pastor") will be leaving soon for an upgrade.

Ironically, achieving the title "senior pastor" is always seen as a promotion even if the new church and circle of influence is much smaller than in the "associate" days. Apparently, there is a lot of power in the word *senior*. So I decided to change our nomenclature.

We changed my associate's title to match mine. We now had two "senior pastors." Though nothing changed in terms of what he did, the congregation's perception and response to him changed remarkably and almost immediately. So did his self-perception.

The questions and the pressure to get his "own church" stopped. People began to turn to him for things they previously seemed to think that only I could answer or do. Twenty years later, he finally left to "get his own church." During the twenty years he was with us, he helped our church grow numerically and spiritually in ways it never could have if he'd been forced to fly elsewhere.

Today, we have four "senior pastors." It drives outsiders nuts. (They can't figure out who's in charge.) But our people love it, and so do the senior pastors. As for role confusion, it doesn't create any more role confusion than having multiple partners in a law firm or business venture. We all know our roles. But we also all share a platform that says loud and clear, "I'm not the only important person around here."

What titles you can and can't share within your polity will vary. But titles are powerful platforms that cost nothing to give away except a willingness to share some of your own organizational prestige and power with others.

Roles

Another powerful way to platform others is to allow them to do things that send a signal of spiritual authority within the context of your church traditions and organizational culture.

Weddings, funerals, baptisms, preaching, and up-front leadership at special events provide significant platforming opportunities. Letting others take the lead in these situations sends a strong message, as long as two conditions are met: (1) *They do a good job at it.* A stumbling or embarrassing performance in the spotlight helps no one. It doesn't platform someone; it devalues them. (2) *They aren't seen as a substitute.* If the only opportunity to take the lead happens when I'm out of town, it doesn't platform someone; it positions them as an understudy.

Our church is so large now that no one knows if I'm at another venue or campus, out of town, or in the audience — or even sleeping in, for that matter. But up until we reached a few thousand in attendance, I made sure I was highly visible whenever I wanted to platform someone.

For instance, when I first started sharing the pulpit, I would come back from vacation a day early, make announcements, and sit in the congregation taking notes. Since no one knew I'd been on vacation (I didn't broadcast it to the congregation), my presence told people that this was our "other teaching pastor," not my substitute.

Another platforming example would be my decision years ago to have our worship pastor start presiding over communion. Previously, I would step in and take over after he had led us in worship and prepared our hearts. But by doing so, I unintentionally conveyed that I alone was spiritually qualified to lead the congregation in the Lord's Supper. So one week I asked him to transition us directly from worship into communion while I sat in the congregation and partook along with everyone else.

Once again, it immediately elevated his stock, since up to that point, our church tradition had always been to have the top dog step in and take over.

Now, years later, the culture of our church has changed radically. The Lord's Supper takes place in all of our small groups at the end of each quarter. It's led by lay leaders, so presiding over communion no longer carries the same symbolic status.

And that illustrates an important point about platforming: Each church and faith tradition has its own symbols of spiritual prestige and power. They can change over time. You have to figure out your own. But once you begin to see your ministry and staff through the "platforming lens," you'll be surprised at how many places a subtle change in title, role, or actions can send a powerful message to young eagles and others that they don't have to go elsewhere to become a "real pastor" and fly.

2. Are Young Eagles in the Loop or in the Meeting?

Another key to keeping young eagles and releasing them to have significant impact is to make sure that they aren't just kept in the loop. They also need to be in the meeting. The distinction between the two (and the importance of it) is something I learned while serving in my first full-time ministry position.

I was the young eagle.

The church was a large Baptist church, one of the two or three largest in the denomination. Though I was only twenty-four years old, I had somehow landed the job as the youth pastor. I was treated unbelievably well. I had an excellent salary and strong support. I was even given the opportunity to preach. Before long, I became the second-string preacher, which meant preaching when the senior pastor was out of town or not too many people were expected to show up (Labor Day, Memorial Day, and all the other "where is everybody?" Sundays, for example). Even so, it was a great honor because I was nowhere near that high on our organizational food chain.

Best of all, the senior pastor consistently brought me into the loop on churchwide programming and ministry decisions. He not only told me what was happening; he asked me what I thought, he listened, and when appropriate, he incorporated my advice.

I couldn't believe my good fortune. I knew I was being honored and empowered far beyond anything I had a right to expect. My wife and I loved the area, the church, and the people. We even bought a house.

Only one thing was lacking. Despite my access to the senior pastor and the decision-making process, I was never in the room when a final decision was made. I waited outside the door like a good little eagle while the pastor, the deacons, and a few key staff members made the final call.

In one sense, there was nothing wrong with that. I had no right to be in the room. But nothing said "cage" like sitting outside the door wondering what was going on in there.

So within a couple of years, I did what all young eagles do when they feel locked out (or locked in). I flew the coop.

To everyone's surprise, I took a cut in pay to become the pastor of a tiny church a fraction of the size of my youth group. It wasn't that I wanted to leave. It was that I needed to fly. So I traded the comfort of a nicely feathered cage for a small shoebox without a lid.

That's what young eagles do when we confuse *keeping them in the loop* with *inviting them into the meeting*.

3. Who Gets to Ride Shotgun?

One of the surest ways to put a ceiling on your ministry is to fill leadership roles on a first-come, first-served basis. Yet that's exactly what many of us do. Whether it's a seat on the board or an influential role on the staff, the first person to get there gets to stay there. New folks and young eagles are expected to take their place in queue and wait until something opens up.

It reminds me of a game I used to play with my friends. Whenever a group of us jumped into a car or van to go somewhere, the first person to cry out "Shotgun!" got to ride in the front seat.

That works fine for a road trip. But the problem with churches playing shotgun, is that the ride goes on forever.

Shotgun churches are easy to recognize. Just look for a church where all the good and influential seats on the leadership bus are filled by old-timers. And the telltale sign is a once thriving church that has grown old, nostalgic, and culturally irrelevant. Still another indicator is a strong youth ministry but few young singles or young families in the worship service. (I call these "feeder churches" because they feed the fast-growing churches in town with a steady stream of young eagles, singles, and families.)

When tenure is the primary determiner of who sits where on the leadership bus, a church is headed for trouble. There's no way it can effectively utilize or keep its young eagles. Nothing crushes the spirit of a young eagle like the realization that there won't be any room at the top until someone who's already there dies off.

Just this week I talked to a frustrated young leader in a once great church that is now slowly dying. As I listened, he lamented an environment that marginalizes young leaders without even knowing it. At thirty-five, he's trusted with an important task, well paid, and given lots of affirmation. But a place at the leadership table? No way. He's far too young and inexperienced for that (though last I looked, he is old enough to be president of the United States).

Ironically, this church's present leaders (both board and staff) were all in their late thirties to early forties when they took the reins and led the church into its heyday of growth and relevance. But much like my high school buddies, they're convinced that the new crop of freshmen will never measure up to their own wisdom and prowess.

They'd love to keep this young staff member around. They love his gifts. They love him. They can't imagine why he'd leave such a "great church." But there is no way he'll stay. They've already crushed his spirit. They've already lost his heart. He just hasn't packed his bags yet.

Biting the Bullet

All this stuff about making room for young eagles and others makes for nice theory. But it's very difficult to pull off. Those who already have a good seat on the leadership bus are seldom cooperative when asked to sit somewhere else, especially when it's for a younger person who ought to wait their turn.

As a leader, my choice is clear. Either I can slowly kill off the future of our ministry by allowing tenure to determine who sits where, or I can bite the bullet and start moving people around.

There is no easy or pain-free way to do it. Asking someone to move to another seat almost always leads to frustration, hurt feelings, and ruffled feathers. Sometimes the hurt is so great that the lay leader or staff member will decide to get off the bus or find another church. But it has to be done. There is no other way to make room at the top. No one ever decides to change seats on their own.

I remember a few years ago when we added a highly gifted teaching pastor to our team. A few of our key staff members weren't too thrilled about it. One even told him during the interview process that if *he* were in charge, we wouldn't be adding him to our staff.

One of our elders also wasn't too keen about putting this pastor on the elder board. He told me, "He's too young; he's only in his midthirties. He needs to prove himself and get some seasoning before we add him to the board."

I quickly pointed out to the concerned elder that *he* was in his early thirties when he became an elder, and I was twenty-eight when I became his senior pastor. It was a classic case of the freshmen getting smaller.

Fortunately, our staff members and elders alike acquiesced and welcomed our new teaching pastor with open arms. Almost immediately, he began to infuse our ministry with a fresh wind of insight, enthusiasm, and new ideas — none of which would have been heard or heeded if he'd been forced to sit at the kids' table.

Before he came, we were already successfully reaching a younger demographic. After he came, our ability to do so was accelerated.

That's what happens when young eagles are allowed to sit in some of the best and most influential seats on your leadership bus. Though it is never easy, it seems like every time I've asked someone to move over to squeeze someone new in, the pain and pushback on the front end has been well worth the rewards on the back end.

Toward a Cure: Zero-Based Retreats

Besides giving our young eagles a good seat on the leadership bus, one of the best ways I've found to make sure that they have significant influence is to periodically host what we call a *zero-based retreat*.

This is simply a small leadership retreat, during which we ask the following types of questions:

- What would we do differently if we were starting all over again?
- What are we doing now that we wouldn't do?
- What are we not doing now that we would do?
- On a scale of 1 – 10, how effective is each ministry and program?
- On a scale of 1 – 10, how effective is each staff member?

If done right, a zero-based retreat is a great way to make sure that your young eagles have major input. I like to keep it small (six to eight is the ideal number). And I don't invite people to participate based on where they are on our organizational chart; I invite them based on their ability to help us dream creatively and wisely about the future. And ideally, half of the room is forty or younger.

It's amazing how differently a group with a significant number of thirty- and forty-year-olds sees life and ministry. If only one or two young eagles are in the room, it's easy to blow them off. Put critical mass in the room and it's hard to hold them back.

One way or another, young eagles will fly. It's our choice as to where. If your leadership team chooses to shut them out, please don't complain when they fly down the street and plant a church that sucks away all the kids, young families, and energetic folks who used to join you for Sunday services.

Part 2

EQUIPPED FOR MINISTRY

Getting Everyone on the Same Page

There are lots of ways to win a game. But no team can win if every player chooses his own game plan.

It's the same in the church. There are lots of ways to do church. But none of them work until everyone is aligned to the same mission, vision, and methods. Getting everyone on the same page is one of the most difficult and important roles of leadership.

Chapter 9

Equipped to Lead

Lobbying Isn't Training

EARLY ON IN MY ministry, I made a big mistake. In my efforts to get everyone on the same page, I confused *lobbying* with *training*.

It's a common error. Faced with a major decision, golden opportunity, or a new vision we want people to adopt, many of us pull out all the stops to make sure that everyone has the same information we have, in the hope that they will come to the same conclusion we have.

But our timing is all wrong.

We may think we're training people. We may think we're giving them essential information. But they know better.

They're being lobbied.

And almost everyone responds to a lobbyist with the same reaction: a healthy dose of skepticism and resistance. This goes a long way toward explaining why so many pastors feel that their best ideas are their most-resisted ideas.

I first learned the difference between lobbying and training when we were about to hire our first full-time associate. I had someone in mind, a member of our church who I knew would hit the ground running. I also knew that every expert on church leadership recommended that we hire for growth rather than wait until the need became acute.

I figured it was an ideal time to instruct our board about the advantages of hiring within and staffing for growth. I put together a packet of all the literature I could find on the subject, sent it out, and asked everyone to be prepared to discuss it at our next meeting.

When we began our discussion, Jim spoke first. "Thanks for the helpful articles, Larry," he said. "But I know there is always another side to every issue. All these articles agree with you. I'd like to see some from the other side as well."

When I told him I didn't have any, that as far as I knew all the experts shared the same opinion, he looked at me with disbelief. He thought I was lying. It took a long time to convince him otherwise.

I learned a valuable lesson that night. *When information is presented too close to a decision-making process, most people will view it as a lobbying effort, not as a training exercise.*

Yet that's precisely what many pastors and leaders do. We store up our knowledge and insights until we think they're needed. We search through our books, conference notes, and old files to gather everything we have on the subject. Then we present it in the hope of swaying everyone to make the right decision, which of course agrees with our decision.

When people don't agree, we become frustrated by their lack of understanding. We wonder why they don't get it, especially in light of all the valuable information we just presented. But that's not how others see it. They don't feel informed; they feel pressured. They don't feel trained; they feel lobbied. And no one likes to be pushed or lobbied into a decision they aren't sure of.

The Danger of Educational Separation

To make matters worse, most boards and staffs suffer from some degree of *educational separation*. This is an organizational disease that occurs when a leader has significantly more education and training than everyone else.

In most churches, the senior pastor has extensive theological and ministry training. The board has little to none; same with many staff members. That often results in differing perspectives and dueling paradigms, which can quickly turn constructive debate into irreconcilable differences. At its worst, this dynamic produces arrogant pastors and distrusting lay leaders.

When I first came to North Coast Church, educational separation was a major contributor to the conflict the board and I experienced. We saw most things from different points of view. The board members had leadership skills and training, but it was all in the context of the secular marketplace. That was the lens through which they saw everything.

On the other hand, I was overdosed with information about leading a local church. Along with my formal education, I continually read books on the subject and attended a host of conferences. But with every book I read and every conference I attended, I became increasingly distanced from the rest of my team, unintentionally creating an ever-widening gap between the way I viewed the church and the way they viewed it.

Rather than becoming a better pastor, I became a cynical pastor — exasperated by how little those who had their hands on the wheel and wallet of our church (and their feet on the brakes) understood about the unique dynamics of leading a local church ministry.

Not sure what to do about it, I decided to try to close the gap. In a context separate from our business meetings, I began to share with the board all the things I was learning. I had no idea if they'd be interested or if it would work. But I knew something had to change or we'd never get where God wanted us to go.

I was shocked. It worked beyond my wildest imaginations. It made me feel like a fool for not having done it sooner. It not only got us on the same page; it made it easy for us to stay there.

Here's what I did and what I learned in the process.

Equipped to *Lead*

In my effort to share with the board all the things I was learning, the first thing I did was change my focus. Previously, whenever I taught or instructed our leaders, I aimed at their hearts. Most everything was of a devotional nature.

But now I aimed at their role. Armed with the new goal of equipping our board members for their specific job as church leaders, I began to teach and convey the leadership principles others had poured into me. When we explored the Scriptures, I zeroed in on leadership passages. When I went to a conference, I came back and taught everyone what I'd learned. When I read a great book, I followed up by having all of us read and discuss it together.

Almost immediately, the gap in our perceptions began to close. Now that the board members were being exposed to the same things pastors and church leaders were being exposed to, they began to think like pastors and church leaders. Even when we disagreed, we started from the same backlog of information and experiences. It became much easier to understand and appreciate each other's viewpoint. Most important, we made better-informed and wiser decisions.

But I didn't change my focus just for practical reasons. I also did it for biblical reasons.

Ephesians 4:11–13 is a popular text and can be found on many bulletin covers, letterheads, and logos. It calls Christian leaders to equip the entire body of Christ for the work of the ministry. It implies that the one-man show is out, that we all have a role to fill, that we need to be trained and equipped to fulfill it.

Yet there I was spending all of my time trying to take the spiritual cream of the crop deeper in their walk with God, while ignoring the one thing they most needed instruction in: how to do the job God had called them to do.

Now, I'm not saying that a deeper walk with God is unimportant. All I'm saying is that knowing how to lead is a rather important skill set for a leader, and it's one thing we ought not leave to chance.

Counterintuitive Leadership

One reason we can't leave leadership training to chance is that ministry leadership for both board and staff members is often counterintuitive. As in almost any field, the seemingly obvious solutions are often the wrong solutions.

Some of the most important keys to developing a healthy and thriving church run counter to conventional wisdom. We might call them the paradoxes of ministry. We've already seen some of them in earlier pages. Things like letting squeaky wheels squeak, avoiding surveys, counting the yes votes, and not worrying about buy-in.

On the surface, these and the other paradoxes of ministry all appear to be dead wrong. But in real life, they work, resulting in faster-growing, healthier, and stronger churches.

It's beyond the scope of this book to list or discuss all the principles and axioms that make for a good church leader. But they aren't hard to find. Any cursory look through your old conference notes or the many books on ministry and leadership that come out each year will reveal the kind of things that lay leaders and staff members need to know but will never know if someone doesn't take the time to teach and expose them to the best practices and key principles of leadership.

It reminds me of a series of meetings I had with a successful, fast-rising copywriter for a local advertising firm. Jim was an obvious expert in the art of persuasion. I knew that if people didn't respond to his appeals, he didn't eat. He appeared to be rather well fed. So I was anxious to hear what he had to say.

For a couple of weeks, we met at a local restaurant. I took notes as he unfolded the basic principles behind modern advertising. When we came to his particular area of expertise, direct mail, I was dumbfounded. Almost all of his advice ran directly counter to what I considered to be common sense.

For instance, he taught me that longer letters were more likely to be read than shorter ones; that a casual, conversational tone far outsold a polished style that would impress your high school English teacher; that a P.S. was the most important part of any letter; and that fancy fonts, while they might look cool, guaranteed that no one would read through to the end.

I was surprised and embarrassed. Most of my congregational letters had been short, polished, void of a P.S., and printed in a fancy font so they looked nice.

My lessons with Jim not only taught me how to become a better persuader and writer; they also sensitized me to how often the seemingly obvious thing to do is the wrong thing to do, which is why lay leaders and staff members need to be constantly exposed to the counterintuitive principles and best practices of church leadership. It's highly unlikely that they'll figure them out on their own.

I sure didn't.

Make It Special

I've also found that it's best, if possible, to set apart special times for training rather than tacking it on to the front end of a business meeting or weekly staff meeting.

When training is tacked onto the beginning of a meeting, it sends a signal to some folks that it is merely the preliminaries before the real meeting starts. You'll find more people tuning out and less people completing any preparatory reading or assignment.

If that's all you can do, it's better than no training. But highlighting your training with a separate meeting tells everyone, "This is important."

With our board, we meet once a month on a Saturday morning for a no-votes-allowed meeting. It's been the perfect environment to teach and discuss ministry principles.

With our staff, we've created special training events (luncheons and half-day meetings) where I, or someone else teaches on ministry and leadership. We've covered everything from the theology of the church, to classic church growth principles, to personality profiles and learning styles. I've even walked our key staff members through the same course material that I teach in doctoral courses at the seminary level.

Time to Reflect

As we've already seen, training that is too close to the decision-making process comes off as lobbying. When training board and staff members, the farther you can get away from a decision-making environment, the better. After all, lots of us do our best thinking on the way home from a meeting.

By exposing your board and staff to ministry principles that have nothing to do with today's issue or decision, you'll greatly increase the odds that they will have enough time to mull over the principles, reflect on them, and even change their mind about them. And when that happens, people don't just have information; they develop convictions.

I think of John, one of our longtime elders. He's a Bible guy. By nature, he's suspicious of church leadership principles that don't come with a verse attached.

When he was first exposed to some of the practical principles I was teaching, he rejected them a priori. "Frankly, this stuff disturbs me," he said at the beginning of one meeting. "We're supposed to be a church, not a business. All these guys care about is numbers."

But with the passage of time, further exposure, and the chance to reflect, John worked through his initial concerns and became one of our strongest advocates for good management principles.

Frankly, if John's first exposure to these principles had been in the context of a decision the board was making, he'd still reject them today. The pressure to act would have felt too much like lobbying for him to let his guard down. He would have had no time to digest the information or to ponder how well it fit with Scripture. Worse, forced to accept or reject the ideas right then, he would have taken a public stand that would be very hard to move from later. Once we take a public stand on an issue, few of us ever change our mind. It's too threatening to our egos. We become so concerned about defending our viewpoints that we have no time or energy to inspect them.

That's why anything you can do to keep your training for ministry from looking or feeling like lobbying goes a long way toward helping people to buy into or reject the ideas on their own merits.

The Process Is More Important Than the Curriculum

Pastors are often surprised to hear me say that when it comes to training board members and staff members, the actual material doesn't matter as much as the process.

It's not that the material doesn't matter. But if there were only one universal set of detailed organizational and leadership principles that guaranteed ministry success, I'd expect we'd find it spelled out in the Bible, not in a twenty-first-century treatise on ministry.

For over two thousand years, Jesus has built his church without any universally agreed-upon polity or philosophy of ministry. In fact, the very things that one great spiritual leader swears by, another great ministry leader swears at. This leads me to believe that we have lots of freedom when it comes to the details of how we organize and get the job done.

That's why I don't worry too much about putting together an ideal curriculum (and why I don't like to recommend any specific material; it can become outdated too quickly). No matter what material I use or even develop myself, it's the process that matters most. Working through the ideas and principles together has far more value than the actual information shared. It creates a shared pool of information and experiences that puts everyone on the same page. As a result, even when we disagree, we at least know what we're disagreeing about.

Frankly, I tend to put most of my leadership training together on the fly. I rarely do it more than a few months ahead of time. I prefer to do it this way for a couple of reasons.

First, I don't know the future. While I don't want to get so close to a decision that I come off as a lobbyist, I do want to address the issues that I see on the horizon. And I want to maximize teachable moments as they occur. So I prefer to keep my options open rather than be locked into a set curriculum and schedule.

Second, I want everyone to view ministry and leadership training as a lifelong process. Curriculums have a beginning and an end. They're usually viewed as something to finish. Once we're done, we think we're trained. That's the last thing I want our board and staff members to think. We can't afford to stop learning and growing.

In short, the demands on our board and staff constantly change. New and unforeseen challenges and opportunities crop up. I've found that a highly flexible training program is a great way to guarantee that the training of the board and staff will actually relate to their current tasks.

Never Confuse Familiarity with Understanding

A final word about training and equipping: training needs repetition, lots of it. Yet most training covers an item once and then moves on.

We tend to think that once we've covered a topic fully, everyone understands. We forget that most people need to hear, think about, and discuss a new concept several times before it soaks in. But as teachers and leaders, we can fear boring people so much that we move on long before the lesson has been learned.

We confuse familiarity with understanding.

To keep from doing that, I try to keep in mind the three stages of learning: *exposure, familiarity,* and *understanding.*

Stage 1: Exposure

Exposure is by far the most exciting stage. It's energizing to have an "aha" moment. It's fun to be exposed to new ideas and to wrestle with concepts and principles for the first time. For those of us who teach or train others, this is the stage at which we receive the most positive feedback, so it's often the stage we prefer to live in. But at this point, no one has really learned anything yet. They've only heard a bunch of new and exciting stuff.

Stage 2: Familiarity

Familiarity is the stage at which a few people in the room start to tune out. The really bright ones remember the ideas and know ahead of time where the discussion is going. Their eyes glaze over and their body language shouts, "I've heard this before."

This is the point at which many pastors bail out. In the fear of putting someone to sleep, we anxiously search for something new and fresh we can expose people to.

While I'm certainly not advocating boring teaching, I am advocating that we not let a few bright people who get it the first time short-circuit the learning of the vast majority who need to hear and discuss something multiple times before they get it.

The truth is that many of those who are most certain they got it the first time didn't get it at all. They're just familiar with the concept. They recognize it. But they still can't apply it or put it into practice on their own.

Stage 3: Understanding

Understanding doesn't take place until people can fill in the blanks *before* we speak. It's knowing something well enough to apply it and explain it without being prompted. It's a stage at which few people arrive because no one ever takes them there.

To bring people to the point of understanding, we need to think of ministry training as something to be dripped into people's lives rather than poured in all at once. We need to approach it more like a glacier than an avalanche.

An avalanche is full of power and fury. It looks impressive. But ten years later, you'd never know it happened. Glaciers, on the other hand, are boring. They look like nothing is happening. But a thousand years later, they leave behind a Yosemite.

Avalanches make a ruckus. Glaciers change the world.

By keeping these three stages in mind, I've been able to avoid the natural temptation to move on from an idea too quickly. It's also helped remind me how quickly we can forget what we once thought we knew.

I don't think my board and staff would classify the process by which we train and equip them for ministry as boring, but they would admit to a few boring moments. It's a price I'm more than willing to pay in exchange for having a team that understands the key principles of leadership rather than simply being familiar with them.

Equipped to Lead Anywhere

Focusing on training and equipping lay leaders and staff members to be better leaders doesn't just pay dividends for the church. It also pays dividends in the marketplace.

I remember when one of our elders called to tell me about a major job promotion he had received. After I congratulated him, he said, "This is a new track for me, but I'm incredibly excited about it. I'm confident that I'm ready for the job, and I owe a lot of that to the training I've received as an elder. I would have never guessed that serving on my church's board would get me a promotion at work."

I'm sure his company would have never guessed either.

It strikes me as ironic that most board members and staff members receive so little training today, because the modern-day senior pastor receives so much. This is the age of continuing education and additional degrees. It's not only encouraged; in many cases, it's required.

If the increasing complexities of modern-day ministry necessitate more training for the "professionals," shouldn't that apply to our key lay leaders and ministry staff as well?

And if I, as pastor, have failed to do my part to train my leaders to lead, what right do I have to complain about the way they do their job or make their decisions?

Chapter 10

Board Alignment
The Power of an Extra "Shepherds' Meeting"

WHEN I BECAME A senior pastor, I wasn't so naïve that I expected board meetings to be the highlight of my ministry schedule. But I didn't expect them to be the low point either.

Yet they clearly were.

As I've already mentioned, I was dismayed by the undertone of distrust that permeated many of our meetings. We squabbled over silly issues like retreads or new tires. We spent way too much time on minutia. Our divergent backgrounds fostered far more misunderstandings than new insights and perspective. Add to that the two board members who felt compelled to make sure I didn't gain too much influence and power, and you can see why I rated board meetings somewhere between a trip to the dentist and a day at the DMV.

And those were the good meetings.

Even worse, we almost completely neglected the weightier things of spiritual leadership: seeking God's vision, dreaming, strategizing, evangelism, discipleship, and extended prayer.

In the board's defense, it wasn't due to their lack of concern about spiritual issues. Much of it had to do with the dysfunctional traditions, structures, and selection process we'd been saddled with. But even after we'd dealt with those things, one other variable made it hard to focus on spiritual issues. We didn't have enough time, and as often happens when time is in short supply, the urgent things crowded out the important things.

Not quite sure how to squeeze these items into a meeting that was already too long, or how to keep them from becoming a perfunctory opening exercise to be rushed through, I hit upon an idea and suggested something I never thought I'd support: *why not schedule an extra monthly meeting to deal exclusively with these important but neglected priorities?*

I called it a "shepherds' meeting," intending to highlight the spiritual and leadership dimension that came with shepherding the flock that God had given us.

I had no clue if it would work or if anyone would agree to come to another meeting. But I asked anyway, positioning these extra meetings as exclusively set aside for three things:

1. Team building
2. Training
3. Prayer

I also promised that no votes or business decisions would take place at these meetings. We'd keep them strictly focused on the bigger picture of ministry, discussing ideas, learning, and praying together. And all of it would be completely free from the pressure of any impending votes or decisions.

The board agreed to give it a shot for six months. But as you might guess, the idea did meet with some low-level passive resistance. Nobody said anything, but a couple of board members obviously saw it as a second-string meeting, as evidenced by their sporadic attendance.

Yet within a year, our absenteeism problems had disappeared. In fact, everyone began to see and treat these shepherds' meetings as equal to, if not more important than, our regular business meetings. The lame excuses vanished.

I knew we'd turned a corner when one board member showed up bleary-eyed after a red-eye flight that had arrived home at 2 a.m.

I asked him, "What are you doing here?"

He said, "I didn't want to miss it."

I gave a subtle knowing nod. He had no idea that on the inside I was jumping for joy like some guy who'd just won the lottery.

It wasn't long until our shepherds' meeting became a permanent fixture. Today, I can't imagine trying to build a healthy and unified lay leadership team without it. It has become the key vehicle for building trust, finding common ground, and deepening relationships. So much so that one former board member took to calling it "our monthly unity meeting."

Why It Works

The beauty of a regularly scheduled nonbusiness meeting is that it provides both me and the board with a regularly scheduled forum for communication, training, and prayer that is unencumbered by competing agendas. I don't have to jam leadership training, healthy discussion, or extended prayer into an already packed meeting.

Instead, I can relax, knowing that no matter how tight our budget might be, how full the agenda looks, or how complex the issues we face, I'll still be guaranteed at least one meeting a month devoted exclusively to these important priorities. And I've discovered that whenever important things get on the schedule, they inevitably get done. They become urgent.

Not a Business Meeting

The secret of a successful shepherds' meeting is to differentiate it as much as possible from a business meeting.

To keep the distinction sharp, we not only stay away from any votes or decisions; we also keep no minutes. Only in the rare case of a consensus that is quickly reached and so obvious that waiting until our next business meeting would be a ridiculous exercise in legalism do we allow a decision to be made or acted on.

Distinguishing shepherds' meetings from business meetings ensures that my attempts at sharing my perspective or leadership training won't come off as lobbying. It allows our discussion of key issues and concepts to be spared the posturing and lack of genuine listening that usually accompanies the pressure of an impending vote or decision.

Picking the Right Time

We originally held our shepherds' meeting on a Tuesday evening. But I quickly found out that after a long day at work, it was hard for most of our board members to gear up for a spirited discussion, in-depth training, or extended prayer.

So we started meeting once a month on a Saturday morning. We almost always meet in a home because we found restaurants hindered our candor. Even when we met in a separate room, the inability to retire to a more casual environment for discussion or prayer crimped what we were trying to accomplish.

During breakfast we swap stories, catch up on news, and renew our friendships. Then we move into a time of training, interaction, or prayer that lasts anywhere from an hour to an hour and a half. I also use this time to candidly share with the board what is going on in my own life and family.

Over the years, the topics of discussion and the formality of our training have changed based on the makeup of the board and the issues we were facing. When the church was smaller and the board was less connected and experienced, we were far more structured than we are today. But the key to a successful shepherds' meeting is not found in the topics we cover or in the way we cover them. It's found in finding a time when the business agenda is out of sight and our board members' natural energy level is high enough to allow for candid and thoughtful discussion of whatever issues we choose to tackle.

More Time Equals a Closer Team

The quickest benefit of a shepherds' meeting is a closer team. As we've already seen, simply spending more time together almost always results in a closer bond.

When that extra time is used to develop a shared set of experiences, vocabulary, and discussion points, it makes getting on the same page far easier. And in the case of inevitable disagreements, it enables everyone to more quickly understand where the other person is coming from and to more successfully navigate the landmines that come with strong disagreements.

The same goes for extended prayer. It not only produces spiritual benefits; it also produces relational benefits. Something about coming before our heavenly Father dissipates spiritual sibling rivalries. It's hard to fight with a prayer partner.

The development of these closer ties had an immediate and significant impact on our business meetings. The meetings quickly lost their confrontational edge. We still had our differences, but at least now we disagreed as friends.

Our meetings also became much shorter. Even today, despite the complexity of being a megachurch with multiple campuses and well over twenty worship services each weekend, most of our board meetings last less than two hours.

Separate Meetings Equals Better Training

A separate shepherds' meeting also makes training more effective. It positions the discussion of ministry and leadership concepts as something important enough to merit a dedicated time slot. That alone tends to dramatically increase focus and follow-through on any special reading assignments or projects.

I discovered why while doing research for my doctoral dissertation. I interviewed a group of senior pastors to find out how many were intentionally training their board members. My goal was to discover the real-world impact of such training. To my surprise, most of the pastors who claimed they trained their board had board members who said they received no training.

At first, I couldn't figure it out. The pastors gave me detailed descriptions of when, what, and how they were training their board members. But the board members said they'd never been trained. How could that be?

Then I noticed something interesting. In all the churches where the pastor thought he was training the board but the board members felt they weren't being trained, the pastors were trying to train them at the beginning of a business meeting or were in some other way tacking training on to an existing program. Apparently, this caused their board members to view it as an obligatory opening exercise, so they sloughed it off as insignificant and unnoteworthy.

A separate shepherds' meeting also harnesses the power of on-the-job training. I used to think that the best way to train people was to do it on the front end, well before they started whatever it was they were going to do. But I've changed my mind. I'm convinced that in most cases the best training is on-the-job training. It offers immediate application. It has a quicker learning curve. More important, those who are already on the front line know what's important and what's not. They're not tempted by esoteric and idealistic theories. They want to know what works.

Whenever I teach a course at the seminary level, I can quickly tell who's already serving in ministry and who's preparing to serve someday in the future. Those on the front lines aren't too concerned about the differences between infralapsarianism, supralapsarianism, and a Labrador retriever. Those who aren't there yet often think it's the most important question in the world.

That's why, given the choice, I'll always choose on-the-job training over front-loaded classes or curriculum. Leadership is not an academic subject. It's an art and skill that's best learned in a hands-on environment.

Another reason for choosing on-the-job training is that the board is already in place well before most pastors (except for church planters) arrive. On-the-job training is the only kind of training that can be done immediately. Putting together a prerequisite set of hoops to jump through and a curriculum for prospective board members to work through before joining the board is a process that, at best, will take years to put together, get approved, and actually walk people through.

It's incredibly inefficient.

It's a nice theory.

But it never works in the real world.

Separate Meetings Equals Unrushed Prayer

A separate shepherds' meeting also provides adequate time for unhurried and extended prayer. Until we added this extra meeting, only the biggest emergencies drove us to extended prayer.

Occasionally, I'd try to set some time aside for prayer at the beginning of a business meeting. But it never worked. It was a big deal if we spent five minutes praying; ten minutes was a revival. More often, we simply replaced seeking God with prayer's popular substitute: an "opening word" of prayer.

But once we had a special time and place set aside for prayer, things changed. There was no longer a subtle pressure to rush; no one was worried about dragging out a meeting that was already too long. We actually talked to God about stuff.

To guide us, we followed some basic guidelines.

First, we limited the time spent sharing requests. It was too easy to spend thirty minutes talking about what to pray for and ten minutes praying, so we decided to bring up most requests while we prayed. If something needed an explanation, we explained it in the prayer. If some of us needed further clarification, we interrupted and asked for it.

Second, we prayed conversationally. We asked everyone to pray for no more than one item at a time. That kept our long-winded prayer warriors from putting everyone else to sleep while they rambled on.

Third, we prayed for individuals by name, candidly and specifically. Group prayer can be awfully generic. Since we wanted to make sure that we didn't skirt the real issues, we prayed for anyone whom we saw in need of God's help. It didn't matter if our perception of the need was rumor, intuition, or hard facts. I'd rather find out we had prayed for a false alarm than fail to pray because the need hadn't yet become acute enough to be public knowledge.

Obviously, with this kind of candor, there's a potential for gossip and slander. That's why I wouldn't recommend this approach for a large group or a spiritually immature board. But once you have the right people on the team and a high level of unity, trust, and maturity, I wouldn't do without it.

We've never been burned. But even if we had been, I'd keep at it. I'll gladly take the risks in exchange for the benefits. After all, prayer is a form of spiritual warfare. I'm not sure it was ever meant to be tame or safe.

Full Disclosure: Time and Growth Change Things

In the interest of full disclosure, it's important to note that with the passage of time and the growth of our church, our shepherds' meetings have gone through some changes in both format and content.

The team-building aspect has not changed at all. These are still our primary "unity meetings." They provide the relational glue that keeps us all connected.

But the training component has morphed into more of a conversation than a presentation. Whereas I used to teach or lead a guided discussion, the process is much less structured today.

For years, we read books on leadership (both secular and Christian, practical and theological) and worked through specific topics and issues. But now, with most of our elders having served a decade or more (some having passed the twenty-year mark), our challenge is no longer how to get everyone on the same page or how to create a set of common experiences and vocabulary. We already have that. The issue today is how to *keep* everyone on the same page. This is a much easier prospect, as long as we continue to meet and discuss ministry and leadership together.

If you were a fly on the wall at one of our current shepherds' meetings, it would seem more like an open-ended discussion than a training session. You might think we were just friends talking about the church and the issues of the day. But in reality, the goal is still the same: equipping our board members for their work in the ministry. I just go about it in a more informal manner, building on the common base of knowledge and experiences we developed years ago.

But the biggest change in our shepherds' meetings has been in the area of extended prayer. Somewhere around the three-thousand attendance mark, our ability to engage in meaningful and intelligent prayer for the congregation began to break down. With even much larger numbers today, our church is simply too large for any of us to know who we were praying for or what the real issues are. Frankly, any attempt at the kind of extended prayer we used to experience would be nothing more than an exercise in pretending we cared.

Sorry if that sounds carnal, but it's true.

It's rather hard to pray for a list of names that have no faces.

As a result, we've pushed prayer for the flock out to our small groups and a team of prayer warriors who take on a specific group within the church. Doing this has enabled us to connect faces with names and to ensure that the thousands of needs and requests that come our way each week are properly and sincerely cared for.

One of the things I miss most about the days when our church was small enough to get my hands around is the time we spent praying for the flock. But there's little I can do about this change. Our church has grown strictly by word of mouth. We do no marketing or advertising. So when God continues to send more people our way, we have to find a way to adjust. We can't just close the doors or hold on to the patterns and practices we liked when the crowds were small. After all, the guy who put up the No Room in the Inn sign is hardly the hero of the story.

But few churches will hit the stage at which prayer for the flock becomes so generic that it needs to be moved to another venue. Until that point, extended and candid prayer for the flock remains an important element of spiritual leadership that is all too often ignored.

Chapter 11

Staff Alignment
Plumb Lines and Assumptions

IN MY EARLY DAYS at North Coast Church, I was the only pastor on staff. That made staff alignment a breeze, at least on most days.

In addition, the next two full-time staff members we added were close friends of mine. We saw not only ministry but most of life through the same lens. Our ministry alignment came so easily that I made a rather foolish assumption. I assumed that staff alignment would happen naturally as long as we all shared a common goal, a genuine love for God, a passion for the lost, and a decent mission statement.

I was wrong.

I found that putting together a church staff can be a lot like gathering a group of friends for a road trip. Just because everyone shares a love of travel, drives the same kind of vehicle, and agrees to observe the traffic laws doesn't mean they'll automatically take the same route to get there.

On the contrary, if someone doesn't step forward to clearly lay out the route and a predetermined schedule, the group won't stay together long. Someone will always opt for the scenic route. Another will choose the most direct. The hyper dogs will want to gulp down coffee and energy drinks while pushing on through the night. Others will insist on eight hours of sleep and regular rest stops as the only way to get there safely.

Now, all of these routes and schedules can work. But if it's supposed to be a group trip, someone has to make sure that everyone knows that on *this* trip, we are following *this* route and *this* schedule.

In many ways, that's the role of a lead pastor with multiple staff members. It's not enough to pull together a team that shares a common theological and philosophical perspective. It's not enough to get everyone dialed in on the same goal. You also have to make sure that everyone understands the route they're supposed to take, the pace, and any special rules of the road.

This is especially true when a new senior pastor inherits an existing staff or brings in staff members from another ministry. When things go bad, it's seldom because of a disagreement about the destination. It's almost always a squabble over the day-to-day itinerary, the pace, or the best route to get from here to there.

Ministry Plumb Lines

The most powerful tool I've found for overcoming these differences and for making sure that my staff is aligned in terms of their day-to-day values and decisions is something I call "ministry plumb lines."

I first started using these years ago in an attempt to find some way to quickly and accurately convey the values and priorities I wanted our staff members to keep in mind when making decisions.

Ministry plumb lines function much like a carpenter's or mason's plumb line. They make sure our programs, ministries, and decisions line up with the core values and priorities we claim to have. And they let everyone know how we are supposed to do things around here.

In a sense, they're organizational proverbs — a list of pithy sayings that describe clearly and concisely what we value and what I expect our staff to think through when making ministry decisions.

How They Work

I have a list of twenty-one ministry plumb lines that I've used over the years to make sure that my decisions reflect my values. I've distilled that list down to ten plumb lines that I share with our pastoral staff to clarify expectations and priorities. And many of our individual programs and ministries have their own set of plumb lines as well.

To see how they work, let's take a look at the plumb lines we currently use to guide our missions ministry.

It's no secret that missions can be a battleground of competing ideas and priorities. Some folks couldn't care less about missions. Others think every dime should go overseas. Worse, once someone gets all geeked up about a particular ministry or mission, they can become a real pain in the backside. It's not unusual for them to whine, complain, and pester the entire staff and anyone else they can corner until they get their way, which usually means jumping on their bandwagon and helping lead their parade.

That's where our plumb lines come into play. Once we've articulated what we're about, it's obvious what aligns and what doesn't. That makes it far easier to resist the persistent parishioner or any small group of single-issue lobbyists who want us to take a different route.

Now, obviously, each church has to figure out and articulate its own plumb lines. You might love our missions plumb lines or hate them. That's not the point. I offer them as an example, not a recipe. But to see how they work and the power they have to clarify and bring about alignment, let's look at North Coast Church's current plumb lines for world missions.

North Coast Church's Plumb Lines for World Missions

1. *Everyone needs Jesus.* Since no one comes to the Father except through Jesus, we will give *top priority* to ministries and missions that actually bring people to Christ rather than those that focus solely on meeting physical needs.

2. *All people are of equal value in the sight of God.* Therefore, we will give *top priority* to ministries and missions where the harvest and return on investment is greatest. We will seek cluck for our buck.
3. *The local church is God's plan A. There is no plan B.* Therefore, we will give *top priority* to ministries and missions that either plant churches or build up existing local churches.
4. *Middlemen just get in the way.* Therefore, we will not function as a middleman filtering communication or doling out financial support. Instead, we will encourage direct contact between our people and the missionaries and organizations they support. This will result in a less impressive missions' budget, but it will produce far greater hands-on kingdom involvement.

Now, even if you think these plumb lines represent the worst possible way to fulfill the Great Commission, they obviously provide clarity for our staff. They communicate how we want options processed. They let everyone know what kind of things we will do and won't do. In essence, they make most decisions a snap, and they remove the strong temptation to give in to the person or organization that applies the greatest pressure or squeals the loudest.

So what does it take to put together a useable set of plumb lines for an entire ministry or a specific program? Here are some of the most important things to keep in mind.

Be Specific

Over the years, I've worked with lots of business leaders as well as pastors. In almost every case, one of the first things I have them do is create a set of personal and company plumb lines.

The first draft is generally useless. That's because it tends to be politically correct — a statement of what the leaders think their vision, values, and passion *ought* to be rather than an honest list of what they actually believe.

I find that pastors and church leaders often do the same thing. Our mission statements and attempts at articulating plumb lines are often so generic and politically correct that everything and everyone can claim to align with them.

The first characteristic of a useful set of plumb lines is that it actually says something. It has to be specific. If it's so generic that two opposite paths can each claim to be aligned to it, it says nothing.

That's not to say that values like "reaching the lost" or "glorifying God" are unimportant. Obviously, they are. But the purpose of plumb lines is to clarify *how* we plan to go about reaching the lost or glorifying God in *this* church at *this* time.

Be Honest

Plumb lines don't represent the *only* way to do ministry. They represent *your* way of doing ministry. So don't worry if they seem somewhat narrow or controversial or even if they thin the herd.

One of the primary purposes of plumb lines is to identify misalignment. If a potential staff member (or current staff member) can't agree with or doesn't want to align to your plumb lines, that doesn't make them a bad person. But it almost certainly makes them a bad hire.

One of the great advantages of plumb lines is that they identify and objectify misalignment long before it becomes acute and messy. Let's look at one of my top-ten ministry plumb lines as an example:

> *Real ministry takes place in small groups.* A crowd is not a church. It's impossible for the biblical "one another's" to be lived out in a large group setting dominated by casual acquaintances. Therefore, the success of our ministry will be determined by the number of people we have in small groups, not the number of people who attend our weekend services.

Now, that's my personal passion and compass. It reflects what God laid on my heart decades ago. I obviously want all of our staff aligned to it. But it's not universal. It's specific to North Coast Church. Lots of great churches successfully take a different route. They could care less about small groups or view them as an ancillary program.

And that's fine. Last I looked, I was neither the Holy Spirit nor the pope. My plumb lines aren't designed for other churches. They're designed for my team. They're an alignment tool, nothing more, nothing less.

That's why you shouldn't worry about what everyone else is doing or what's politically correct when putting your own plumb lines together. If church planting, community service, missions, evangelism, and all the other hot buttons aren't your passion, go ahead and leave them out. Put down what God has written on *your* heart, for *your* ministry, at *this* time.

Otherwise, you'll end up with plumb lines and mission statements that don't honestly reflect the values, assumptions, and behaviors you expect. And they'll end up buried in a drawer somewhere.

Be Different

A great set of plumb lines also highlights any areas of unique vision, perspective, or expectations that you may have.

Effective leaders are almost always a little bit weird. They approach ministry and life a few degrees off center. That's what sets them apart. They see and sense things that others miss.

But sadly, most leaders have no tool to communicate their thought process or the unique values and perspective that drive their decisions. Again, that's where the value of plumb lines comes in. It gives your staff and team something to gauge their own thought processes, assumptions, and decisions by. It gives them a track to run on.

For instance, I'm big on on-the-job training. I value it far more than one-on-one mentoring or an educational model that frontloads information and training. I also distrust long-range planning. I think the only thing we can know for sure about the future is that it will be radically different than what we spent all that time planning for. I believe the best way to reach non-Christians and disciple them to maturity is to make everything we do believer *targeted* and seeker *friendly*. And I'm convinced that most leaders like everything big, while most people like things small. (I've never had a member of our church crave a bigger auditorium, but our speakers and worship leaders would love nothing better.)

All of these are reflections of my unique (some would say weird) approach to ministry. Many are different from how the majority of our staff members would approach things if left on their own. And that's precisely why I include these things in the plumb lines I share with our staff.

The more unique or out of step with conventional wisdom your vision or priorities are, the more important it is that you find a way to articulate them in your plumb lines. Otherwise, no one will know what to align with. And odds are, most of your staff will head off in the wrong direction, completely unaware that they are doing so.

A Coach's Example

I once worked with a young track coach who asked me to help him hone his leadership skills. His unusual passion, drive, and skills made it obvious that he was going to be something special.

But as is often the case with high-performers, he had a hard time getting in touch with and then communicating to others the unique perspective and insights that set him apart. His leadership was so instinctive and intuitive that it was almost impossible for those around him to understand what he was thinking or how to duplicate it.

So we began to work on getting in touch with and then articulating his coaching plumb lines. The first list he came up with was filled with standard clichés. When I asked, "Do you *really* believe this?" he said, "No, not really."

But one statement on his list jumped out at me. It said, "Every athlete should reach the potential he or she *wants* to reach."

When I asked him what he meant by that, he said, "If someone wants to be a champion, then it's my job to push them to a championship level, but if they want to run track, play in the band, and smell the flowers along the way, then it's my job to help them do that to the best of their ability."

Now that was a new one to me. He was the first coach I'd ever heard articulate a desire to help athletes become what they *wanted* to be instead of all they *could* be.

We wrote it down as his first plumb line. It was clear and concise, and it reflected one of the unique values and priorities that guided his approach to coaching. It was also something that no one on his staff would know if he didn't articulate it. It was counterintuitive. If he didn't spell it out, the rest of his coaches and leaders would almost certainly head off in the direction of pushing everyone to reach their full potential, all the while frustrated and angry at the slackers who were satisfied to be less than their best.

His final list included a few other unique and clarifying statements like, "Hard work can and should be surrounded by fun," and, "Our ultimate goal is a lifetime runner, not a high school champion."

By the time we finished, he had a short list of powerful organizing principles that he could share with his staff and his athletes and their parents. It told them what to expect. It told his assistants how to coach. And it explained to everyone why the campouts, parties, and ancillary activities were just as important to him as the workouts.

It's no surprise that his teams grew from a handful of athletes to well over a hundred in just a couple of years, or that they went from the bottom of the pack to competing on a national level, or that my daughter is now a lifetime runner and my son didn't feel guilty about going to the prom the night before a big race — or that one of his athletes became a national champion.

His plumb lines kept everything in alignment. They let everyone know what was important to him, what he expected, and how success would be measured. They ensured that his genius and insights were not only present when he was in the room but also when others were taking the lead. And once it was clear where he was headed and how he planned to get there, it was easy for everyone else to decide if they wanted to jump aboard or not.

What about Mission Statements?

I haven't said much about mission statements. That's not because they aren't valuable. They are. If done well, they point everyone in the same direction. At North Coast Church, we have one: *making disciples in a healthy church environment.* In the next chapter we'll look at it in a little more detail.

It's definitely helped us stay on track by defining what we're aiming at. We've also defined exactly what we mean by a "disciple" and the five vital signs of a healthy church so that we have something to continually judge our progress by.

But having said that, if forced to choose between a great mission statement and a clear set of plumb lines, I'd choose the plumb lines every time. That's because the devil and most disagreements are in the details. I find it relatively easy to get our entire staff headed in the same direction and aiming at the same goal. I find it much more difficult to ensure that everyone is taking the same route to get there.

To my thinking, the greatest value of a mission statement is its ability to keep an organization focused and free from a disease called "mission creep."

For a classic example of mission creep, think of the YMCA. The Young Men's Christian Association was once dedicated to reaching young men for Christ through recreation and athletics. It's now morphed into a Judeo-Christian organization dedicated to improving the community through recreation and athletics. That's mission creep.

But since so much has already been written about mission statements (and since so many are watered down, politically correct, group-think projects that are sitting in a drawer somewhere), let's move on.

The Difference between a Plumb Line and a Wish List

It often surprises people to hear that I don't care if anyone on our staff can articulate our plumb lines from memory. I know I can't.

What I do care about is that our plumb lines are articulated often enough that everyone is familiar with them. I don't want anyone saying, "I've never heard that before."

But I find it unrealistic to expect people to recite them. If I've done my job well, I've dripped them into enough conversations, taught them enough times, and aligned our decisions and actions with them long enough, that they've become part of our corporate culture.

What I want most is whenever someone in our staff or leadership hears one of my plumb lines, they think, "Yes, that's exactly the way we do things around here."

Because otherwise, I don't have plumb lines. I have a wish list.

Chapter 12

Congregational Alignment

Preempting Conflict

YEARS AGO, I CONFRONTED a member of our church as he was putting "Christian" voter guides on all the cars in our parking lot.

I politely asked him to stop.

When he asked why, I explained that our church didn't support any specific candidates, propositions, or ballot measures, and that by placing his voter guides on the cars in the parking lot, it gave the impression that we were supporting the candidates and ballot measures recommended by his voter guide.

He was incredulous. I think he thought I said, "Jesus isn't ever coming back again."

So I explained it once more.

I'm not sure, but I think he still thought I said, "Jesus isn't ever coming back again."

It was hard to tell. Because once he flipped the rage switch, he started yelling something about supporting the devil, communists, foreign automobile makers, killing babies, raising taxes, and directly causing the moral decline of America, as well as advocating sexual perversion and preventing his kids from praying in school (though I'm pretty sure they prayed before they took a test).

I stood there dumbfounded. He'd always seemed like a rational and supportive member of our church. But obviously something changed the moment he realized that I wasn't going to mobilize our congregation to support his "Christian" candidates.

Like a fool, I continued to try to reason with him. I took the voter guide and gave it a once over. It covered eight issues. I noticed that they included the candidates' positions on gun control, taxes, and the ceding of the Panama Canal to Panamanian control.

I assured him that I'd read through my Bible a few times, and I was relatively confident that there was nothing in there about gun control or the Panama Canal — and most the stuff it said about taxes was about paying them. So I wasn't quite sure how any of these were "Christian" issues.

Well, that didn't go over too well either. I think this time he thought I said, "I never believed in Jesus in the first place."

I'll never know for sure, because I never saw him again.

Congregational Alignment

That day I learned an important lesson about congregational alignment. Church members are just like board members. They need to hear what I think about dicey issues ahead of time. Otherwise, whatever I say in the midst of a confrontation will come off as lobbying, and there will be little chance of anyone changing their mind.

Our argument in the parking lot caused me to realize that I had wrongly assumed that alignment around our mission and goals automatically meant agreement about the best methods to get there.

Since then, I've worked hard to make sure that our congregation is as aligned with our vision, values, and methods as the board and staff are. While we'll never have perfect alignment with such a large congregation, there are numerous things I can do to preempt incidents like the parking-lot fiasco.

In particular, I've come to rely on five powerful tools to keep us aligned.

1. A clear and simple mission statement
2. A front-loaded pastor's class
3. The drip method of preaching
4. Sermon-based small groups
5. Short and sweet congregational meetings

1. A Clear and Simple Mission Statement

As we've already seen, North Coast's mission statement is, *Making disciples in a healthy church environment.* Everything we do is geared toward reaching that goal. That means we judge our success by two questions.

1. *How well are we moving people along the continuum of non-Christian to fully obedient Christian?* In other words, are we fulfilling both halves of the Great Commission?
2. *How healthy is our church environment?* Something we measure by looking at our five Ws (word, worship, witness, works, and warmth).

Mission statements do no good if they sit in a drawer somewhere or are so obtuse or politically correct that they say nothing. We intentionally keep ours short and terse. It's much more likely to be remembered and actually used to guide our ministry.

To keep our mission statement in front of our people, we put it on the cover of every church bulletin, talk about it in "Welcome Desserts" and pastor's classes, and even write it on walls. In many ways, it's our North Star.

A simple and clear mission statement is an important first step in congregational alignment. It lets everyone know what you're trying to accomplish.

2. A Front-loaded Pastor's Class

Another thing the blow-up in the parking lot helped me realize is that a doctrinal statement and a clear and simple mission statement are not enough. I needed to find a way to make sure that people who started coming to our church (especially Christians from other churches) understood our values and methods, not just what we did but why we did it that way.

The gentleman with the voter guide (okay, the raving idiot with the voter guide) had attended our church for over a year. He assumed we did things just like the church he'd come from because we both taught the Bible, shared a common doctrinal perspective, and used all the same buzzwords.

It wasn't until our little encounter in the parking lot that he realized that we were using different dictionaries and strategies.

Looking back, much of the confusion was my fault. I knew that new Christians needed lots of training, but I assumed those who were already Christians would pick up our values and methods by osmosis. Instead, they tended to interpret everything we said or did through the lens and dictionary of their past church experiences.

To counteract that, and to do any necessary thinning of the herd on the front end rather than after people had settled in, I started teaching a pastor's class subtitled "Why we do, what we do, the way we do it."

We push this class as a get-to-know-us class for those who are new to the church. We're careful not to position it as a membership class since that would scare away most newcomers.

I teach the class, and we cover about five hours of material plus time for questions and fellowship. When the church was smaller, I taught it at my home on Sunday nights. Now I teach it on three consecutive Monday nights at the church.

The goal is to tell people right off the bat why we do, what we do, the way we do it. For not-yet Christians, it's a chance to look behind the curtain. For longtime Christians, it's a great way to pre-empt future conflict by letting them know up front exactly what we are about.

One of my original purposes was to thin the herd on the front end. But to my surprise, that seldom happens. Instead, in the non-pressurized environment of an informational class, most people understand and accept the way we do things.

Take the issue of politics and voter guides, for example. When I start to explain why we don't let our church get hijacked by any political agenda, I can tell by the crossed arms, body language, and the push-back questions that lots of folks don't agree. (And who knows, I might be wrong; someday I'll ask Jesus.) But by the end of our discussion, the room is usually filled with nodding heads. There is something about the casual environment of the class that makes it far easier to consider an alternative viewpoint than if our first discussion of the subject takes place in the church parking lot.

The subjects covered in this type of class will vary from church to church. You might make a big deal about why the church *should* take on political issues. It's your call and your vision. But the key to congregational alignment is to cover the kind of issues that have the greatest potential for misunderstanding on the front end, long before people have settled in with inaccurate assumptions.

As a point of reference, here's a quick flyby of the subjects I cover.

The first evening, I review our mission statement — what it means and how we measure our success or failure in fulfilling it.

The second evening, I cover what I call my "seven hobbyhorses." These are the values and themes that I tend to harp on, the stuff that makes me pound the table. For me, that means explaining things like why we have such a passion for character and an equal distaste for legalism, why we don't jump on every bandwagon that comes down the turnpike (and why we don't fret too much about the latest crisis du jour or passionately support the latest this-will-save-the-world campaign), or why we are so radically biblical when the Scriptures speak and so silent when they don't.

These aren't all of my hobbyhorses. But it gives you a feel for the class. I find that most gifted leaders have a unique set of pound-the-table issues. Letting people in on them as soon as possible preempts competing agendas and increases congregational alignment.

The last evening, I tell the history of our church. It's a story filled with God's fingerprints and perfect timing. It's something most folks would never hear otherwise. It always pumps people up. It lets them see that this is a place where God has been showing up for a long time.

A final ingredient of the class is an opportunity for people to ask me any question they want, from theological to personal. Each session, I take questions people write down on cards and answer them. It makes each class unique and ensures that I have a chance to address any hot-button issues that someone might bring to the class.

3. The Drip Method of Preaching

A third way I try to align our congregation is through the weekend messages. Preaching is perhaps the most important vision-casting tool a pastor has at his disposal. The values and principles taught from the pulpit eventually establish the DNA of a church.

When I first started out, I thought the best way to cast vision was with an annual vision message. I assumed it would get everyone on the same page at the same time. But try as I might, I could never get everyone there, and by the third year, some folks were tuning out, convinced that they'd heard it all before.

By my fourth year, I gave up on the annual vision message and started to approach casting vision in much the same way I approach equipping leaders to lead. Rather than blasting it all at once, I drip vision and core values into every sermon I preach.

The result has been far greater congregational alignment. Dripping core values and vision into every sermon makes them unavoidable. Anyone who would have missed my vision series or who would have tuned out because they'd heard it before is now stuck. Each week I plant a seed or two and then move on, long before they have a chance to tune out or put up their guard. And if they missed this week's sermon, I'll get them next week.

Some things are simply too important to waste on one sermon or sermon series. They are better dripped into everything.

4. Sermon-Based Small Groups

As you may know, our church is built around sermon-based small groups. It's a lecture-lab model in which the groups dig deeper into the subject of the previous weekend's message. For over two decades, we've had a participation rate of over 80 percent of our weekend adult attendance.

One of the great advantages of this approach is that it aligns our congregation around the contents of each sermon. It takes the drip method and amplifies it exponentially.

My first church experiences were close to information overload. I heard a sermon on Sunday, studied a different subject in Sunday school, listened to a third message on Sunday night, and then came back to study a fourth subject during a midweek service or home Bible study.

I'm not sure I ever could tell you what we were studying (something from the Bible, I guess). It all blurred together. Everything was too diluted to remember.

In contrast, our sermon-based model sharpens churchwide focus by making sure that everyone is on the same page. My book *Sticky Church* covers this model in great detail, so for now, suffice it to say that it's been a powerful tool for congregational alignment.[12]

5. Short and Sweet Congregational Meetings

Now, you might be thinking that congregational meetings are hardly a tool for congregational alignment, that they are more like a giant pothole with the potential to throw everything out of whack.

You're right.

But if your denominational polity calls for congregational meetings (as mine does), like it or not, you are stuck with them.

By the way, I'm not as down on congregationalism as the above might sound. I actually like it that our congregation (as a priesthood of believers) has the ability to cast out leaders if they should go wrong or doctrinally shift away from Scripture. What troubles me is the way that congregationalism has been structured and expressed in many churches.

Frankly, the typical pattern of an open mic, detailed information, and voting on lots of things can work pretty well in a church of seventy-five to a little over one hundred adults (which, by the way, was the size of the typical congregation when congregationalism dug its deepest roots). At that size, this approach offers a vehicle for both accountability and transparency. But in today's larger churches (and many are quite large), that old-school style of doing business and making decisions isn't a source of accountability and transparency. It's a platform for malcontents and self-appointed watchdogs to raise a ruckus. You know the type. They insist on reviewing every decision and going over every nickel in the budget with a fine-tooth comb, insisting that every expenditure or ministry decision meets with their personal approval.

To keep that from happening and yet stay faithful to our polity of congregational government, we redesigned the process so that it retained its upside (accountability and open communication) while minimizing its downside (petty squabbles, angry pronouncements, and morons with a microphone).

If your church doesn't have a congregational polity, you can skip the rest of this chapter. But if you do have some form of congregational government, here are some things we've done to keep our annual business meetings from tearing apart our church.

How One Church Does Annual Business Meetings

When deciding how to conduct our annual business meetings, the first thing we did was get rid of anything that resembled a so-called town meeting. I find that the churches that structure their meetings like an open forum have far more disunity than those that don't.

Though intended to be a vehicle for building consensus, in reality, this type of meeting has a strong polarizing effect. It's usually attended by a small percentage of the congregation, most often by those who already have a dog in the fight. It doesn't tend to moderate positions; it tends to harden them.

We also radically changed the format of our annual business meeting. To take the microphone out of the hands of chronic complainers and malcontents, we decided to stretch our annual meeting into a three-week marathon. Instead of having one long night filled with presentations, questions, discussion, and then finally a vote, we set it up so that we had three weeks of open discussion followed by a brief meeting at which the only thing we did was vote.

For the three weeks prior to our annual meeting, elders are available at each campus after each service. That gives people ample opportunity to ask any questions, get information, or make suggestions. It even gives them time to lobby others if they want to.

But on the night of the meeting, we open in prayer, pass out the ballots, take a vote, and go home. The whole process takes ten to fifteen minutes.

Frankly, not many people show up. But that's a sign of high trust, not low commitment (the measure of commitment is best found in our high number of volunteers, not in how few show up for a boring business meeting).

I remember the first time we did it this way. After I prayed and we started to pass out the ballots, one man spoke up and asked, "Aren't we going to have some discussion?"

I looked at him and said, "We've had three weeks of discussion. As promised, tonight all we're going to do is vote."

He didn't know what to do. He was a chronic whiner. He always had something negative to say. But without a microphone and a captive audience, he suddenly had no power or influence. With a resigned shrug of his shoulders, he sat down. I almost busted out laughing, but my filter took over. I put on the best stoic face I could muster.

Still, I think he knew.

By maintaining this process year after year, we've been able to remain faithful to our tradition of ultimate congregational authority. But we've also busted the tradition of turning every little disagreement into a full-blown church fight by taking one of the worst sources of congregational misalignment and filling in the potholes.

Part 3

COMMUNICATION

Keeping Everyone on the Same Page

Getting on the same page is one thing. Staying there is quite another, because mission tends to creep and vision tends to leak.

One thing that distinguishes great teams is the way they navigate the landmines and danger zones that bring so many other teams down.

Chapter 13

Change Diplomacy

Minimizing Conflict and Chaos

DURING MY FIRST THREE years at North Coast (a time frame that I still call the "dark years"), I developed a Pavlov's-dog response to the phone. Just one ring and I'd feel sick to my stomach.

I'd been trained by a steady stream of negative calls to expect the worst. It usually began with someone from the congregation saying, "Hi pastor, I want you to know that I love you in the Lord, but ..."

Instinctively, I'd brace myself, having learned that "I love you in the Lord" is Christian code for, "You're not going to like what I have to say next."

And then they'd let me have it.

Most often, it was for a serious moral lapse or leadership failure — like the time I discontinued the tradition (two years strong at the time) of holding an all-church New Year's Eve party, or the time I curtailed our open-mic sharing because if I had to listen to Dave ask for prayer for his sister's next-door neighbor's best friend one more time, I was certain I would lose it, or the time I stopped using Nicky for special music because it wasn't so special and her voice made the kids cry.

At first I thought perhaps our church was simply more mean-spirited, petty, and carnal than most. But I quickly realized I wasn't alone. Most pastors experience the same thing and have their own battle scars, horror stories, and "been there, done that" T-shirts to prove it.

An Old Farmer's Advice

It reminds me of the advice an old farmer once gave to the young and newly arrived pastor of his church. "Go slow, son," he said. "Churches are a lot like horses. They don't like to be startled or surprised. It causes deviant behavior."

He was right.

Our fiercest battles are seldom fought over theology. They're fought over change, especially any change that comes as a surprise, alters a comfortable tradition, or represents a symbolic changing of the guard.

I know of one nearby church that has been engaged in a perpetual war zone for nearly twenty years over what name to use on their big sign out front. It keeps changing every few years, which makes it easy to figure out who's got the current upper hand. All you have to do is check for the presence or absence of the word *Baptist*.

I think of another church I know of that lost over twenty families when the pastor had the audacity to remove a historic (read that as about fifteen years old), oversized marble pulpit and replace it with a music stand. He was a short guy and had to stand on a box to see the first few rows of the people he was preaching to. Unfortunately, no one told him that the family who had donated the money for it and the craftsman who had built it were related to a lot of other families in the church, none of whom cared if they could see him or not.

Frankly, there was a time when such "deviant behavior" left me angry and cynical about both Christians and the church. I wondered what it was that made us so particularly resistant to change.

But I was myopic.

Resistance to change is not a Christian problem. It's a human problem. Almost any group, Christian or secular, has a strong bias toward protecting the past and sustaining the status quo. Even people who pride themselves on liking lots of change and mixing things up tend to favor the changes they make, not those imposed on them by others.

Once I realized that our resistance to change was more sociological and psychological than spiritual, I quit bemoaning my congregation's lack of spiritual openness and started dealing with it as a leadership issue. I changed my tactics. I began to look for ways to minimize rather than completely remove resistance, and I began to focus on improving my communication patterns.

In particular, I started to follow a four-step process that I still use today when introducing any significant change or innovation to our board, staff, or congregation. It's a process that I've found significantly reduces the kind of "deviant behavior" the old farmer warned me about. Here it is.

Step 1: Test the Waters

The first thing I want to do with a new idea, potential change, or innovation is to find some way to gauge how people will respond. I call it "testing the waters." I do something political leaders are masters at.

Long before making a major proposal, they leak a rough sketch of it and then stand back and analyze how the press, their constituents, and their opponents respond. Was the idea vehemently rejected? Widely praised? Which points did opponents attack? Which criticisms were legitimate, and which were obviously partisan? And most important, what changes are needed before making the proposal official?

In a similar vein, I like to ask a cross section of our people — board members, staff members, unofficial power brokers, and regular folks — what they think early on in the change process.

But I always ask them in smaller, informal settings where the conversation is free-flowing and easy. I don't want anyone to feel that they are being lobbied. I don't want anyone to think I'm making a proposal. And I certainly don't want anyone to hold back their initial thoughts and feelings.

At this point, I'm not trying to get buy-in or permission; I'm not trying to garner support or build a coalition. All I want is a quick reading of people's initial reaction to the basic idea. By testing the waters in casual conversations or some other clearly exploratory environment, I get invaluable information.

First, testing the waters lets me know whether my dissatisfaction with the status quo is shared by others. If not, it's time to slow down and help others see the need or risk of being on the wrong end of some "deviant behavior."

Second, testing the waters tells me what changes not to make. For instance, when our church was founded, it was named for the city we met in. When we moved to a nearby city, everyone agreed the name had to be changed. I also wanted to drop the denominational tag. I felt that in our community, having a church name that included any denominational affiliation was a huge negative, far more likely to keep people away than to draw anyone in.

Most people seemed to agree. But while testing the waters I discovered some strong opposition from a couple of key elders and lay leaders who would have fought the idea tooth and nail. So I dropped it. Major conflict and a church split was a price I was unwilling to pay for such a minor victory. Testing the waters had saved my tail. A few years later, another test of the waters revealed that no one cared anymore, so we became North Coast Church.

Third, testing the waters tells me what parts of a proposed change will receive the strongest resistance and who will be the staunchest resisters. Knowing that allows me to more accurately count the cost and consider any potential fallout ahead of time. It lets me know if an idea is DOA or simply needs to be reframed and reworked. But most important, it makes possible the next step: listening and responding to resisters early on in the process.

Step 2: Listen and Respond to Resisters

Leaders often look upon resisters as adversaries. Sometimes they are, but usually it's a case of mistaken identity.

Rather than view those who initially resist my ideas as enemies to be overcome, I prefer to see them as advisers helping me to transform a good idea into a great idea. Like pain in our physical body, these resisters let me know where something is wrong or slightly out of whack.

Resisters have an uncanny ability to point out *all* the potential flaws within a proposal. After all, they're motivated. They're superb at finding any weaknesses or hidden defects. By listening carefully, I can learn exactly where a change or new innovation is most likely to go wrong, saving me lots of unnecessary midcourse corrections.

For instance, at the five-year mark of our ministry, we wanted to make home fellowships the axis of our ministry. That meant canceling most other programs and putting all of our stock into what was at that time an unknown quantity. And soon afterward, we moved farther into uncharted waters with sermon-based small groups, a lecture-lab model that takes the weekend message and digs into it more deeply.

Tying our small groups to the sermon was an excellent idea that would revolutionize our church and eventually spread to churches across the nation. But before we started, many bugs had to be worked out of our idea. The initial resisters helped us identify and fix them long before we rolled out our first groups. We couldn't have gotten better information if we'd hired a bunch of high-priced consultants.

Our resisters told us that lots of people feared being stuck in geographical groupings in which they would have little in common with others except their neighborhood. They worried about studies that would be no more than a sharing of ignorance or a regurgitation of the sermon. They fretted over being asked to share too deeply too quickly. And they absolutely hated the idea of being asked to divide their group after they'd started to bond. In short, they set an agenda of things for us to work on.

Our listening and responding to their concerns didn't win everyone over. Some folks still dug in their heels. But listening and responding did help us put together a far better small group ministry, one that has thrived for decades.

Here's something else early resisters can point out: hidden psychological barriers. Sometimes a change or innovation fails not because it's a bad idea but because of the way it's presented, what it's called, or some other issue that has nothing to do with concept itself.

To identify these psychological barriers, I ask myself two questions.

1. Are resisters objecting to the proposal or to the presenter? Pious-sounding objections can cover up the real source of resistance: a lack of trust in the person presenting the idea. Newly arrived pastors often have to deal with this type of resistance, particularly when the church has a history of short pastorates.

The same goes for a pastor who has alienated a segment of the congregation or a couple of board members. Their resistance often has nothing to do with the proposal itself; it has to do with the presenter.

If that's the case, it's a waste of time to keep on pitching your idea. Instead, it's time to focus on restoring relationships and building trust. And if that can't be done, it's wise to find someone else to champion your proposal.

2. Are resisters objecting to the proposal or to the way it's presented? This is a common problem. Lots of good ideas and changes are resisted because they are presented with offensive language — not swearwords but loaded terms and phrases that carry a negative connotation to the listeners.

For instance, while serving as a youth pastor, I suggested an internship program to disciple young men and women planning to go into full-time ministry. Since our church was near a seminary and two Christian colleges, I figured the idea would go over big. It didn't. The board rejected it without discussion.

When I sought to understand why, I discovered that my predecessor had been fired for focusing his ministry on a small group of disciples at the expense of everyone else. As a result, words like *discipleship* and *intern* conjured up images of narrow favoritism. By using those terms in my proposal, I had unwittingly torpedoed my idea. The board wasn't against training young people for future ministry; they opposed the abuses of the past.

So I reframed the proposal as VMTP (short for Vocational Ministry Training Program). Now, that's a terrible name, cryptic as an acronym and terminally boring in its long form. But within a month, not only did I have my program (by unanimous consent); I also had twice the funding I'd requested.

While I don't want to grant every critic veto power or a strong hand on the steering wheel, I do want to know what they think. For the most part, they are good and intelligent people with legitimate concerns or an honest difference of opinion. Listening and responding to any early resistance that surfaces during the testing-the-waters stage always results in a better idea and a lot less resistance later.

Step 3: Sell Your Idea to Individuals before Groups

The third step in effective change diplomacy is to sell your idea to individuals first. Before bringing a new idea or proposed change to the congregation, staff, or board, I always want to have some strong supporters lined up first.

This is perhaps one of the most neglected principles of group persuasion. We don't do it for a variety of reasons. Sometimes it's because we don't want to come off as manipulative, or we don't want to show favoritism, or we're convinced that a great idea will stand on its own merits. But no matter what the reasons are, neglecting this step is always a big mistake.

Years ago, I saw a painful illustration of this when I watched a long-range planning committee present its findings and proposals at a special congregational meeting. The committee members had spent nearly two years of prayer, research, and hard work hammering out the details. Their presentation was beautifully done. Their proposals were well thought out and much needed. But the congregation rejected their plans outright.

The pastor and committee members were devastated. They had assumed that a clear presentation of an excellent idea would automatically result in widespread approval. But that's not how groups decide what to support and what to reject. The pastor and his planning committee had made two critical mistakes.

1. They put people in the awkward position of going public with their initial reactions. By presenting the proposal to the entire church, the committee had practically guaranteed its rejection because initial reactions to change are most often negative, and few people ever back down once they've gone public with their opinion.

2. They ignored the fact that most people won't adopt or support a change until they know who else is for it. The long-range planning committee assumed the only relevant question was, "Is this a good idea?" They failed to realize that only a small percent of people (about 15 percent) will ask that question first. Almost everyone else asks, "Who else is for it?" and then decides if something is a good idea or not.

The committee did good work, but its members were mostly folks who were not widely known. No one had broad-based credibility. So when people started to ask tough questions, they had no one but themselves to step forward and defend their proposal. That caused many in the congregation to decide that there must be something wrong with the idea.

Lining up some visible support before the meeting would have changed everything. It would have given their ideas instant credibility. That's why I always try to sell a new idea to a few individuals before bringing it to our board, staff, or congregation — just in case they want to know, "Is anyone else for it?"

But even if all of these steps are carefully followed, there will still always be some resistance. At times it will be fierce. I'm convinced that some folks in my church would vote against the second coming if given a chance. I'm sure they have a few relatives in your church as well, which is why this final step in the change-diplomacy process is so important.

Step 4: Lead Boldly

Once I've tested the waters, listened and responded to the legitimate concerns of resisters, and sold the idea to a few individuals, it's time to lead boldly. I don't mean running roughshod over those who disagree with me. I do mean stepping forward to forcefully champion a cause, clearly making my views known and doing everything I can to persuade the holdouts to follow.

For many of us, this type of leadership doesn't come easily. It runs counter to our image of the pastor as a gentle shepherd. It forces people to act or react. It can offend dear old saints or longtime supporters. It can drive people away, sometimes in large numbers.

Yet without bold leadership, nothing will get done. Inertia will rule. Those who let a few upset people (be they staff, board, or congregational members) put a halt to much-needed changes end up with a ministry that resembles a bus with one accelerator and sixty sets of brakes.

While it's never wise to allow a handful of critics to hold off an army of supporters, how boldly to lead depends on a variety of factors.

First, *Is it God's will?* Unfortunately, God's will is not always as clear as we'd like. Sometimes I'm not sure if my latest vision is from God or last night's pizza. The more unsure I am, the less boldly I lead.

But even when I'm absolutely convinced that something is God's will, I check one more thing: *is this God's timing?* I've learned that God's will has a *what* and a *when.* The question of timing is often answered during the testing-the-waters stage.

Once I'm convinced that something is God's will and that we're within his timetable, I'll charge the hill with a water pistol. In those rare cases when he's actually spoken to me about something, I'm not afraid to pull out the heavy artillery and publicly state, "This is what God wants us to do." But I always triple check to make sure that it was God, not the pizza, because I know I only get one chance to misplay the "God told me" card. After that, my credibility would be pretty much shot, and for good reason.

A second consideration is, *What price will I have to pay for this act of bold leadership?* Assuming that God hasn't unmistakably said, "Charge that hill," only a fool fails to count the cost before going to war (at least that's what Jesus said, and I've found he's pretty smart about stuff like that).

If the price is too high, and God hasn't unequivocally said, "Charge the hill," bold leadership isn't a sign of valor; it's a sign of stupidity.

The third question I ask myself is, *Who will we lose?* Notice, I don't ask *if* we will lose people; I ask *who* will we lose. No ministry can keep everybody happy. Losing some folks is unavoidable. The only question is who those people will be.

Take worship music and ambiance as a case in point. In case you haven't heard, a few churches have had some minor disagreements over music and atmosphere. While I prefer offering multiple options (thus our commitment to video venues and multisite campuses), most churches can't do that. They have to settle on one option or another. Whatever choice they make is guaranteed to push some people away and draw others closer. It's unavoidable. When there is no such thing as a win-win, someone always loses. It's one of the tough jobs of leadership to choose who that will be.

Numerous times in our history I've championed changes that I knew would cause some of our current attenders to go elsewhere. But, each time, I was convinced that a failure to act would cost us even more in terms of the people we couldn't reach (and keep) if we didn't make the changes.

Most often, I've been willing to lose those who want to hold on to the past at the expense of creating the future. I know that these folks won't have a hard time finding another church in town that fits their cultural preferences. So I'll let them go in order to reach the people that few others are reaching.

Your choice of who to lose might be different than mine. But one thing is certain: whatever we choose to do or not do always determines who we can and can't reach. That's why when it comes to choosing between change and the status quo, the right question is never, "Will we lose some people?" The right question is always, "Who will we lose, and are these the people we're willing to lose?"

The final question I ask before pushing through a major change is, *How long do I plan to be around after the change is made*?

If your answer is, "Not long," please don't push too hard.

I have a friend who accepted a call to a small, struggling church a few years ago. While the church had potential, it wasn't going anywhere without some major changes. So he pushed them through, altering the style of the worship services, canning programs, and changing the staff around. Though difficult and costly in the loss of a few families, the changes allowed the church to begin to grow for the first time in decades.

The only problem was that he didn't stay long enough to solidify the changes. Not long after the changes were made, he left. When he returned to visit just a few years later, he was disappointed to find that most of his changes had been reversed. The worship service, atmosphere, and low attendance were strikingly similar to what he had encountered when he first arrived.

Leading boldly requires a commitment to stay. Change is always difficult, no matter how great the gains might be. Why send a body of believers through pain and loss of equilibrium if we aren't going to be around to help them regain their balance? Why risk driving away key old-timers if we aren't going to be around long enough to help the new folks dig in roots and gain a sense of ownership?

I look at it this way. If I won't be around to pick up the pieces, it's not a good idea to start breaking the old dishes. No matter how nice the new china I just bought might be.

○

Over the years, North Coast Church has gone through some huge changes. I often tell people that in terms of style and corporate culture, we've been three completely different churches during my tenure. Not that our message has ever changed; it hasn't. And not that we've turned over or lost lots of people with a revolving-door ministry; fact is, our back door has remained relatively small.

Nonetheless, we've changed a lot. I've gone from suits with monogrammed shirts, to Dockers, to flip-flops and jeans. We've morphed from searching for excellence to thriving in an atmosphere of laid-back authenticity. Our outreach methods have changed from special "bring-your-friends-to-church" events to massive service projects that send our people out to minister in the community. And we've gone from being a small everybody-knows-everybody church to being one with multiple campuses and worship venues that feature everything from gray hair and hymns to body art and giant subwoofers.

Yet all of these changes have been accomplished without even one massive exodus or church split. Outside of my first three years at North Coast, when I did everything wrong and learned most of the lessons in this book, we've had no widespread infighting or any of the other gut-wrenching consequences of change done poorly.

Mostly it's because we've carefully navigated the change-diplomacy process outlined in this chapter. It's enabled us to minimize, though not completely remove, unnecessary conflict and the kinds of "deviant behavior" the old farmer warned me about.

Basically, we've been able to build an openness to change into our DNA that is best illustrated by a conversation I had with a man and his family a few years after we'd made a particularly significant churchwide programming change.

He said, "We grew up in a church where every change was a major battle, so we were bummed when a few weeks after we'd decided to settle in, you got up and talked about the changes that were going to take place. We were so worried that we even thought of leaving before the battle broke out. We couldn't believe it when nothing happened. We still can't believe how easily this church accepts change."

Of course, it wasn't nearly as easy as it looked.

But I sure was glad that he saw it that way.

Chapter 14

Setting Salaries

Investment or Expense?

MINISTRY SALARIES ARE A strange thing. The word on the street is that they are notoriously low, but surveys find that many pastors and staff members are quite happy with their pay. In some churches, everyone knows what the staff makes. In others, salaries are a state secret.

Everyone agrees that fair and adequate salaries are important. But outside of an occasional denominational or regional salary survey, most of the people tasked with setting compensation have no context for what's fair, standard practice, or equitable. So they guess, most often using their own jobs as a reference to determine what's reasonable.

To make matters worse, staff salaries are often set late in the night at the end of a long budget meeting, when everyone is weary and anxious to get home. In many cases, the pastor leaves the room while the treasurer suggests salaries he or she feels the budget can handle. After a brief discussion, the board adopts a figure remarkably close to the treasurer's original proposal.

Add to the mix the fact that most pastors and staff members hate to talk about money. Though it can be a real drag to watch your family's financial security rise and fall with the whims of an exhausted board, no one wants to sound like a whiner. No one wants to appear ungrateful. So we end up saying "Thank you," when we really mean, "That's not enough."

The whole thing makes for an awkward situation — kind of like a junior high after-school dance, where all the guys stand up against the wall, desperately wanting to talk and dance with the girls but having no idea how to ask or what to say if one of them ever said yes.

To make the salary dance work (and to increase staff morale, longevity, and honest communication), both sides usually have to learn some new steps. To start with, let's take a look at the pastor's and staff's responsibility to speak the truth, even if the truth is uncomfortable.

Honest Feedback

When I arrived at North Coast Church, I discovered that one man held the offices of board chairman, finance elder, and treasurer. He was also the driving force behind our fledgling building program (even though we had less than a hundred adults attending). His number one priority was to save enough money to purchase property, which explains why I had to take a significant cut in pay from my old youth-ministry job to become his pastor.

I realized rather quickly that I'd better learn some negotiation skills. If I didn't, we would have our little building and I'd need a second job.

Yet like many pastors, I absolutely hated the idea of talking about money. I cringed at the thought of a fund-raising event. I especially despised talking about my own compensation. It just felt wrong — "yucky" is probably the right word. It made me want to take a shower.

But I had no choice.

Keeping silent was not only unfair to my family; it was unfair to the board. Whether I was comfortable or not, I owed it to them to be as forthright and honest as I expected them to be with me. And I had no right complaining to my spouse or friends if I hadn't first let the board in on my concerns.

And that's the first law of fair and equitable compensation: *everyone has to be honest.* It's a "speak now or forever hold your peace" kind of deal.

Certainly, there are a few situations in which honesty may not be the best policy. For instance, when you're faced with a deeply divided board or a one-man thorn in the flesh. In such cases, it's better to start with your supporters than your enemies. But frankly, such situations are not all that common.

Most boards are made up of good people who want nothing more than to faithfully serve God and support their pastor and staff. But they can't make fully informed decisions if they aren't fully informed or if their pastor and staff hold back. It's not a sign of spirituality to keep quiet. It's disingenuous (which is a modern-day politicians' fancy word for "dishonest").

Too Much Is Seldom a Good Thing

Board members also need to learn some new steps. One of the first is to take into account the complex relationship between salaries and morale.

Contrary to what most people think, high salaries don't increase morale. They just increase expectations. Low salaries, on the other hand, kill morale — especially when they are perceived to be below what our peers in the same field make.[13]

That's why I always tell my board and our executive pastor that the goal is to pay our top people one dollar more than their peers make. Above that, there's no upside. If you've ever received a big raise, you know what I mean. Think back to how you responded. It probably felt great for a few months. But after that, it was simply a new baseline.

Setting Fair Salaries

To help our board settle on the right amount for salaries, we sometimes use the standard salary surveys. But more important, we try to keep these four important principles in mind.

1. Always Compare Apples with Apples

Many unfair compensation packages are the result of not knowing how to accurately compare a pastoral salary with a layperson's salary.

Most board members have no idea of the true cost of their salary. If asked, they will give you an amount. But it will seldom include the actual cost to their employer. Most forget about medical insurance, payroll taxes, retirement, continuing education, and other benefits.

Yet when board members or church members look at a pastor's or staff member's salary, they often look at the total cost to the church, not the amount that they actually receive.

When I first arrived at my church, our budget had a category titled "Pastor." It included my salary, housing allowance, and medical insurance. It also included mileage, entertainment reimbursements, professional dues, subscriptions, the cost of attending conferences, continuing education, and a book allowance.

That made everyone think I was doing pretty well. But in reality, as I mentioned earlier, I had taken a significant cut in pay to become their "overpaid" pastor.

The best way to keep that from happening is to simply create two budget categories: one for salaries and one for benefits, payroll taxes, and the like. And when you discuss staff salaries, never combine these two categories. This will ensure that everyone is comparing apples with apples.

2. Establish Replacement Value

An obvious key question when setting salaries is, "What can we afford?" It's what any prudent leader wants to know. But it should never be the first question asked. The first question to ask is, *What would it cost to replace this person with someone of equal skills and abilities?* Only after that question has been answered and duly noted is it time to ask, "What can we afford?"

Replacement cost sets an objective standard. It tells us what the marketplace will bear. It removes the subjectivity that can result in paying someone too much or too little.

It also helps to deter staff turnover. Anytime someone is paid significantly below replacement cost, chances are they know it. Odds are, they won't be around too long.

Assuming it's a pastor or staff member that we want to keep, it's always shortsighted to pay less than it will cost for their replacement. Employee turnover is always fraught with hidden costs: moving expenses, training, and lost productivity. In the church, it usually results in a significant loss of momentum, if not church-wide, then certainly within the framework of the affected program or ministry.

It's just not worth saving a few dollars.

Another reason to use replacement cost as your standard is that it can help put a lid on salaries that have gotten out of line on the high side. For instance, if a staff member has moved to another role, or if a long-tenured staff member's annual-merit and cost-of-living increases have priced them beyond the role they are currently in, asking the replacement-cost question will make that obvious.

While there may be plenty of reasons to pay someone a premium for longevity, it's important for everyone (including the staff member) to realize that their salary includes a longevity premium. Otherwise, when their ministry position "tops out" as far as salary is concerned, you'll have hurt feelings all around.

Discovering replacement cost is easy. All you have to do is ask yourself who you would try to hire if a key staff member left, then ascertain that person's current salary and benefits.

Finally, in the case of a staff member who's doing a bang-up job, knowing replacement cost helps us slap on some "golden handcuffs." Paying a little more than the going rate not only sends a strong message of affirmation; it also ensures that one of our key players won't be tempted to leave just because someone comes along with a better financial offer.

I don't mind losing key staff members when they are heeding God's call. I hate losing them because we unintentionally made the grass look greener elsewhere.

3. Benchmark Parallel Responsibilities

Though nowhere near as important as replacement value, another consideration when setting salaries is, *What secular jobs parallel this position in responsibility, education, and the skills needed for success?* Though this is a rather subjective question, it can help avoid gross inequities. But it's important to make sure the parallels are actually parallel.

For instance, I talked to a church planter whose board decided his job was similar to a schoolteacher's. So they called the school board to find out what a second-year teacher made. Unfortunately, they failed to factor in educational credits and the fact that a teacher's contract covers only part of the year. What they thought was a comparable situation in reality had little in common with their pastor's job.

Assuming we get the parallel secular jobs right, it's also important to remember that as a church grows, the parallels change.

For instance, some youth pastors have a job much like a camp counselor, others serve in a ministry setting that approximates a high school teacher, and others function more like a school administrator.

The same holds true for a senior pastor. Depending on the size of the church and the complexity of the ministry, a pastor's role might parallel a schoolteacher, a principal, a superintendent of schools, or a company president.

4. Decide What You'll Do If More Money Comes In

Church budgets are notoriously tight. That's why it's also important to decide ahead of time what you will do in regard to staff salaries if more money than expected comes in.

Consider how most church budgets and salaries are set. Once they're established, no one goes back and adjusts them again until the next year. Even when what we can afford changes, nothing changes.

It reminds me of the predicament a friend faced after taking a ministry position in a small, struggling church. His starting pay was deplorable. But it was all the church could afford, so he accepted it gladly. He's a gifted and catalytic leader, so his area of ministry began to grow immediately. So did the church — and the annual budget.

Though my friend got regular raises, no one ever went back and asked what he would be making if he'd started out with a decent salary. Unable to ever catch up to a fair salary, he left for another church a few years later. Only then did the board ask and discover what his position was worth. They were shocked when they found out how much more it would cost to bring in someone else just like him.

It's not that they didn't have the money. They had it all along. But each year when more came in than was expected, they had used it for all the "urgent" needs that cropped up as a result of the increased attendance that my friend helped to produce.

Because they'd never established what they'd do if their finances were better than expected, the urgent things got taken care of while the important things were overlooked.

An inadequate salary is always costly, but sometimes it's all we can do. When that's the case, it's important to clearly establish ahead of time what we will do if more money actually comes in. Otherwise, we'll quickly forget and spend it elsewhere. But I guarantee you, our staff members will not suffer the same kind of amnesia.

Investment or Expense?

Another common financial mistake is to view staff members as an expense. If we hire the right people, they aren't an expense. They're an investment.

Good hires should pay for themselves quickly. Otherwise, the job calls for a volunteer. To put it in business terms, adding a staff member should increase your ministry outreach. It should result in more people, which results in more income.

Certainly, there are times and situations when a particular outreach or ministry will be an intentional loss leader. But no ministry can have more than a couple of these without going broke. As a businessman once told me, "Cash flow is more important than your mother."

I think he overstated it.

I know my mom does. But you get what I mean.

That doesn't mean that ministries that don't pay for themselves should be shut down. It simply means they should be staffed by volunteers, not paid staff.

Here's how to figure out if a particular staff role is an expense or an investment.

- Determine your average annual income per attendee. To do this, divide your annual income by your average annual attendance.
- Now look at any ministry or program. Determine the number of people it brings into the church and multiply that number by your average annual income per attendee. That tells you the theoretical income stream for that area of ministry.
- Subtract from the theoretical income stream the staffing and programming cost to run that area of ministry.

You now have the information you need to know if a staffing role is paying for itself, subsidizing other ministries, or drowning in red ink.

In our case, due to the overhead costs of our buildings, weekend worship services, and administration, I like to keep the expenses of any ministry program at around 50 percent of its theoretical income stream. You'll have to figure out your own ratios. But this is a quick and easy way to discover which staff members are growing our church and which ones are draining the budget.

By the way, I can always tell when a pastor, board, or church doesn't understand that staff members are an investment, not an expense. They ask me, "What percentage of our budget should be spent on staffing?"

My answer is always the same: "I wish I could spend 100 percent of our budget on staffing."

After all, it's people who do ministry, not buildings. Mortgages, utility bills, and programming expenses are a necessary evil. We can't do without them. If given the choice, I'd always rather add more staff than build more buildings. But once they bring in all those extra people, we have to have somewhere to put them.

Chapter 15

Talking about Money

Assumptions, Facts, and a Savings Account

WHEN IT COMES TO money, I'm amazed at how many boards, leadership teams, and churches fly blind.

Expenditures are carefully scrutinized, but where the money to pay these expenditures comes from is anybody's guess. Budgets are often set by tacking an arbitrary percentage on to last year's numbers. Key donors are unknown and unappreciated. All the while, other ministries (colleges, seminaries, missionaries, and parachurch organizations) play by a different set of rules. It's as if the church is supposed to play with one hand tied behind its back.

The results are tight budgets, crimped ministry, and a demoralized congregation and staff.

It doesn't take lots of money to build a great ministry and a healthy team. But it's hard to have either one when margins are so tight that there's no wiggle room, income projections are based on assumptions rather than facts, and key donors are unknown and unappreciated.

Here are some of the most significant things I've learned over the years about handling money, making financial decisions, and responding to those whose generosity makes it all possible.

You'll find that some of these concepts are controversial. Not everyone will agree. I once stridently held some opposing viewpoints myself. But over time, my study of the Scriptures and my observations of life brought me to some new conclusions. I encourage you and your team to consider them with an open mind and to hold them up to the light of Scripture and your own real-life experiences.

It's Not a Sin to Have a Savings Account

I'm intrigued by how many Christians think good stewardship means that their church should spend every dime that comes in. If *too much* money comes in, they seem to feel guilty about it. So they quickly find some special project to spend it on or give it away to the mission field or the needy.

It sounds noble. But nothing guarantees a perpetual cash crisis like the absence of a margin in your budget and a cash reserve in your savings account.

Now, I know that some churches hoard cash and sit on a huge nest egg while ministry opportunities pass by year after year. That's sick. It's not what I'm talking about. A massive bank account is not the goal of ministry. But neither is living on the edge without anything in reserve to help weather the predictable storms of life or to seize a golden opportunity.

The Scriptures (especially Proverbs) suggest that it's wise to have something in reserve. Solomon put it this way: "In the house of the wise are stores of choice food and oil, but a foolish man devours all he has."[14]

When we fail to build a margin into the budget or lack the discipline to store up some savings, it practically guarantees that we will have some sort of financial crisis every year and a long history of missed opportunities.

There is one thing I've learned about opportunity and crisis. Neither one ever sends a text message saying they're coming. They just show up. And in the case of opportunity, it never stays around very long.

Over the years, our reserves have helped us jump on the opportunity to buy buildings that suddenly went on sale at an attractive price. For years, we met in warehouse space, so expanding our ministry often required buying an adjoining building or parking lot when it became available. If we'd had nothing in reserve, the bargains would have been long gone by the time we completed a series of special offerings or put together a fund-raising initiative.

The same thing goes for a couple of key staff additions who suddenly became available. Having cash reserves gave us great flexibility.

One word of caution: if you are in a fast-growing church, rapid or sustained growth can mask the lack of a margin. We went through a period when our budget margin shrank back to zero. The rationale was that next year's increase would provide the margin. It always did, but only because we kept growing. It was a dangerous presumption upon the future, something we'd never recommend to our people (nor would a certain author of Scripture named James).[15] It's also something we stopped doing once we came to our senses.

The only downside I see to setting aside a reserve is when it turns into hoarding. The idea of a cushion is not to see how large it can get. It's to set aside a prudent amount for rainy days and unexpected opportunities. After that, any excess should be spent, preferably on capital expansion, nonrecurring expenses, start-up funding (say, for a new multisite campus or church plant), missions, or the needy — however God leads.

Assumptions or Facts?

Churches are goofy. We're the only organization that prides itself on making sure our leaders have no idea where the money comes from.

Imagine a business planning and forecasting without knowing who its key customers are, what they buy, or how much they spend. Or imagine a missionary who has no idea who her supporters are. Or how about a parachurch ministry or Christian college that has no idea who the key donors are?

Yet that's exactly how a lot of churches function. North Coast Church used to be one of them. I was a card-carrying member of the "I don't know who gives what" club. And I was quite proud of it.

I changed my mind when I was challenged to rethink my position and realized four things about pastors and money.

1. *I had a hard time explaining why a pastor is any different from other ministry leaders when it comes to knowing who gives what.* (Think missionaries, parachurch ministries, Christian media, seminaries, and the like.)

2. *I had a hard time explaining why capital campaigns are different.* No one seems to object when the pastor knows about a large gift or commitment to a building project. So how is this different from donations to the general fund?

3. *I found nothing in the Scriptures to support my viewpoint.* Frankly, all the verses I used to use to support staying in the dark could just as well be applied to missionaries or anyone leading a Christian ministry, even the church treasurer for that matter. The idea that I, as a local church pastor, was somehow different simply didn't pass muster.

4. *Even though I took pride in not knowing about our finances, I still made lots of subconscious assumptions.* I couldn't help it. It's human nature. But once I had the facts in hand, I was amazed at how inaccurate most of my assumptions were.

A while back, I was discussing with a group of pastors why knowing the facts is so much better than making assumptions. The very next day I received an email that highlighted the difference.

Our church was being picketed by an out-of-town labor union. Apparently, the union had a dispute with a subcontractor that our general contractor had hired to help build our new campus.

The union never contacted us. They just showed up — not at the construction site but at our church, during worship services.

They came with a huge sixteen-foot sign that said, "Shame on North Coast Church," with small letters saying, "Labor Dispute," on each end of the sign.

It was an obvious attempt to "motivate" us into forcing the general contractor to get rid of the subcontractor, which by the way, was one of only a handful of nonunion subcontractors on the project.

Anyway, after the first weekend of picketing, I was forwarded an email from a concerned parishioner. The man began by informing us that after prayer and reflection, his family would no longer be giving their "firstfruits" to our ministry. He said he would still give to the Lord what was his, but it just wouldn't be to North Coast, at least not until the issue with the union was resolved.

He then went on to say that though he didn't particularly care for the methods the union was using, he felt our church had a moral obligation to support companies that provide a living wage in order to show the community that we care about people and not just the bottom line. He concluded by thanking us for the way our ministry had blessed his family and promised that they would continue to pray for us as we worked to resolve the issue.

Now, if you were in my shoes, how would you have responded?

Based on the content and tone of his email, my bet is that you would have made the same assumptions that I did. The man was a union member and a strong Christian. He was fully committed to the church, prayed for it regularly, and supported it with his "firstfruits."

If you're like me, you probably would have also wondered (and worried a little bit) about how many other solid families like his were thinking the same thing and, if they were, what they might do.

But here's how I responded.

I asked my assistant to get me some facts. Who was this gentleman? What was his attendance pattern, involvement in our small group ministry, *and* his giving record?

Here's what I found out.

He'd attended our church for a couple of years. He'd never been involved in a small group. His "firstfruits" giving the previous year was all of five hundred dollars. So far, year to date, it was zero.

Now, come on. Let's admit it. That changes things a bit, doesn't it?

Frankly, for me, the facts changed everything. Rather than a response crafted for a strong Christian who was highly committed to our church, the facts called for a totally different response, a response designed for a "big hat, no cattle" Christian who had just made an empty threat about cutting back his nonexistent financial support.

I found myself wondering if he was any relation to Ananias and Sapphira.[16]

My "fact-based" response read something like this:

> Dear———,
>
> Thank you for sharing your concerns about resolving the issue with the protesters. I fully understand in light of your union loyalties why you might be hesitant to give God's "firstfruits" to a church that hires a company in dispute with a union.
>
> Perhaps that's a sign that we are not the best church for you or your family at this time, especially since we're likely to continue to use our donated funds to hire the lowest qualified bidder (rather than the highest bidder) on this and other projects in the future.
>
> In light of your concerns, I've asked our finance department to return to you all the "firstfruits" gifts you have given to our church so far this year. That way you can forward them on to a ministry you can fully support.
>
> Unfortunately, we couldn't find a record of any such gifts.
>
> But rest assured, if we find any, we will send them back to you posthaste. In the meantime, may God guide you and your family as you search for a church worthy of your full spiritual and financial support.
>
> Sincerely,
> Pastor Larry Osborne

Now, did I really send this letter?

That's between him, me, and the Lord.

In the meantime, how are you and your leadership team making your financial decisions? Are you flying blind? Are you crafting plans and determining responses based on assumptions or facts?

Planning for Next Year

Knowing where the money comes from is not only important when it comes to dealing with pretenders. It also plays an important role in planning.

For instance, when the economy or a personal setback negatively impacts a key donor (or when one moves away), it obviously has a major impact on the budget. Yet churches that fly blind in terms of where their money comes from have no way of knowing this until the budget starts to resemble a sinkhole.

The same thing happens when someone gives a large onetime gift. We've had people tithe from inheritances, windfalls, and even game-show winnings. If we were flying blind, we would have no way of knowing that such gifts were onetime donations. Odds are, we'd presume upon them as we planned the next year's budget and then wonder what happened when our income didn't come in as projected.

I recently talked to a pastor who was concerned about a sudden downturn in his weekly offerings. He was in a panic and wondered what it meant. Were lots of people upset? Was it something spiritual? Did he need to preach a stewardship series?

I asked him who his largest donors were. He had no idea. So I asked him to find out if anyone who had previously given large amounts had recently moved, suddenly stopped attending, or had a major financial setback. I pointed out that the appropriate response would be very different if it was due to the loss of one parishioner or if it was a churchwide belt-tightening. It would do no good to hit his people up to restore their giving if the real problem was that the Martins had moved to Florida.

Nowhere to Hide

A final value of knowing where the money comes from is that it smokes out board members, staff members, and leaders who complain about the ministry without being committed to the ministry.

I can't tell you how many times I've talked to a pastor who, upon receiving full access, discovered that his biggest problem board members or staff members had given zero to the ministry, sometimes for years.

In almost every case, once they knew that he knew (or that the rest of the board or top leaders knew), the chronic complainers and obstructionists lost all credibility. Usually, they moved on to another church where they could hide behind a carefully constructed (but blatantly false) image of spiritual maturity and commitment to the church.

It reminds me of one pastor who told me about a staff member who was concerned because she hadn't received any salary increases over the previous couple of years. He told her, "I'm sorry, but too many people give as you give — and until that changes in your life and theirs, an increase in your paycheck is unlikely to happen."

Ouch!

Thanking Donors

Finally, how do you thank your key donors? Or do you? Heaven knows, every other Christian organization is thanking them, profusely.

I'm not talking about rolling out the red carpet when someone shows up in a hot car with lots of bling. I'm not talking about giving big donors a pass on church discipline or an extra hand on your steering wheel.

But what's wrong with a special thank you when a special gift makes a huge difference in our ministry?

I'm not sure how it came about that the spiritual gift of giving became the one spiritual gift that we're not supposed to thank people for or encourage people to grow in. We certainly help our teachers teach better, our mercy folks be more merciful, and our leaders lead better.

We seem to have no problem giving special thanks to an above-and-beyond volunteer, Sunday school worker, or small group leader. In fact, many churches hold banquets to say thank you to these folks.

While I realize that thanking key donors can go overboard, so can lots of things. Too much ice cream will make you fat. But that doesn't mean we throw away the key to the church kitchen.

I've heard all the reasons why pastors and leaders shouldn't do anything special to thank key donors. Remember, I once championed the cause, fearful of the pitfalls of favoritism and manipulation. So for years, we did nothing other than send out an acknowledgment that stated how much someone had given in the past quarter. It was more of an accounting issue than a thank you.

But eventually I came to the conclusion (and so did our board) that these people should be thanked just like everyone else who helps our church accomplish its mission. And just as I was part of the process of thanking everyone else, I needed to be part of the process of thanking these people.

If I can be trusted with the deepest and darkest secrets of our people in counseling, I can probably handle knowing something about their finances. And if I can't handle either one, the church needs to get a new pastor who is spiritually mature enough to know a secret or two.

You may or may not agree with all of the above suggestions. But if not, they are worth some careful consideration by your leadership team. By putting these principles into practice, we're no longer flying blind. We've stopped making decisions based on educated guesses when the facts are readily available. And as a result, we have a more informed board, a better paid staff, grateful donors, and a far healthier congregation.

Chapter 16

When Things Go Wrong

Telling the Truth When the Truth Is Hard

THERE ARE SOME LETTERS you never want to write: a resignation, the sad news of a moral failure, the embarrassing report of a deep financial crisis, the apology for a costly misjudgment, or the release of a well-loved but ineffective staff member, to name a few.

Those kinds of situations are painful for everyone involved.

That's why some leadership teams stick their head in the sand and hope the bad news will go away if they ignore it long enough. It's why others sugarcoat everything with empty euphemisms and God-talk to the point that no one knows what they really mean. But no matter how bad the news is, the best thing a leader and leadership team can do is stand up and tell the truth.

In this final chapter, we'll look at three of the most common "bad news" situations that church leaders have to deal with. If you haven't dealt with them yet, it's almost certain that you will eventually. The big three are moral failure, financial crisis, and the release of a well-loved but ineffective staff member.

Each of these situations is fraught with potential landmines. If handled incorrectly, they can destroy a leader's credibility. If allowed to spin out of control they can tear apart a board, staff, or an entire congregation. But if handled correctly, they can actually strengthen a team and congregation. It all depends on what we do, what we say, and how we say it in the heat and pressure of the moment.

Moral Failure

I'm not sure if anything is more disheartening than the discovery that a trusted spiritual leader has committed a moral failure. The sense of betrayal one feels stems from far more than knowing of the leader's sexual sin; it also stems from all the lies, cover-ups, hypocrisy, and manipulation that accompanied it. You want to believe the best. But in almost every case, the deeper you dig, the uglier it gets.

The first response is usually shock, followed by anger. It's hard to imagine things getting much worse. But they often do, especially when it comes time to figure out how to respond and communicate what just happened.

One of the big surprises is how quickly those who have to make that decision polarize into two camps. Whether it's an elder board, deacon board, presbytery, board of directors, or an executive staff team, you'll find that most people instinctively tend toward one of two paradigms. Some will see everything through the lens of a *family* metaphor. Others will see and respond through a lens of *justice*.

Those who see the situation through a family lens will have a strong bias toward protection. They will want to keep the leader's moral failure under wraps as much as possible, mitigate the consequences, and provide a generous severance and free counseling. They'll also want to make sure that the leader's kids or any innocent parties aren't caught in the backwash. So if that means extending medical coverage, paying to keep the kids in a private school, or some other financial obligation, they'll be all for it.

They will also tend to say things like, "We're a family. We can't shoot our wounded. If we can't model grace and mercy as a staff, what will the congregation think?"

Those who view the situation through the lens of *justice* will see things quite differently. They'll want to expose as much as legally possible. They'll have very little tolerance for a generous severance, extending medical coverage, or anything else that feels like mitigating the consequences. They'll quote Bible verses about teachers coming under stricter judgment and publicly disciplining leaders so that all who see will fear. As for keeping the kids in private school, they'll point to Achan's family and say, "Consider yourselves lucky."[17]

They'll also say things like, "Severance? What do you mean, severance? He's been robbing us for months, taking a salary while living a lie. He's given the enemy a spiritual foothold in our ministry. If we're going to pay for anything, it should be castration, not counseling!"

Now here's the bad news. Under the intense pressure of making a decision as to how to respond (moral failures are not something a leadership team has the luxury of mulling over), most of your leaders will quickly adopt one paradigm or the other, and they won't change their mind no matter how late into the night the meeting goes. And once a decision has been reached, it will almost always be unsatisfactory to one side or the other.

I remember the worst board meeting of my life. A staff member had been caught in a moral failure. As we debated how to respond, one of our key pastors (a personal friend and mentor to the fallen) took up the family paradigm. He felt terrible for the kids, worried about them losing their medical insurance, and wanted us to offer counseling and a lengthy severance.

I, on the other hand, was more on the justice side, though I didn't advocate castration or stoning. The rest of our elders and senior pastors split into the two predictable camps.

Unfortunately, we had to decide something that night. It wasn't as if we could table the issue for a season of prayer and fasting. The clock was ticking. As the meeting spun out of control, there were more raised voices, angry accusations, and hurtful comments than in all the previous meetings we'd ever had.

At one point, it dawned on me that we'd likely lose (literally or emotionally) an elder or two and a staff member no matter which side won. It was a nightmare. As I watched it unfold, I became profoundly angry at the perpetrator. Not only had his sin torn apart his family, life, and ministry; now it was tearing apart our team and ministry as well.

Then it happened. Someone asked if our constitution or bylaws spelled out what to do. They aren't very detailed, so I was sure they didn't. I was right. But they did contain a clause about providing a one-month severance to anyone dismissed for cause. We jumped at it as the solution to our raucous debate, a debate we were never going to resolve ourselves.

I learned a very important lesson that night. You have to decide *ahead of time* exactly how you are going to respond to a moral failure. In the heat of the moment, no one thinks straight. No one compromises.

The division into *family* and *justice* camps is a story I've heard over and over as I meet with pastors. The teams that navigate moral failures best are inevitably the ones that figured out ahead of time what they will do and how they will communicate what happened.

As to whether you should err on the family side, the justice side, or somewhere in the middle, you'll have to make that call. But once you do, it will dictate everything from severance to congregational communication. The key is to decide now so that you don't have to fight later. You'll be glad you did, and so will your team.

Financial Crisis

No one wants to tell people, "We're running out of money." It's embarrassing. It reflects poorly on our past decisions and judgments. It gives ammo to our enemies and sets us up for some legitimate criticism.

But if things have gone south, it has to be done.

Financial crises happen for lots of reasons. Sometimes it's because we fell asleep at the switch. Sometimes it's because we made decisions based on faulty assumptions. Sometimes it's because of something we had no control over. Regardless of the reason, as always, the best policy is to stand up and tell the truth — quickly and clearly, in straightforward language that everyone can understand.

The first thing people ask when informed of a financial crisis is, "How did this happen?"

But what they really mean is, "Why didn't you catch this earlier?"

Answering *that* question and taking *full* responsibility is often the first step toward not only a solution but also regaining trust and credibility.

There are two ways to take responsibility and apologize for something. One is the apology that says, "I am sorry. I take responsibility. But it's not really my fault." It's the apology that we've grown accustomed to hearing from media and political figures who say something offensive and then "apologize" by saying, "*If* I have offended anyone, I am truly sorry."

I always walk away thinking, "Good night, *if* you've offended anyone? What in the world do you think the firestorm was all about?" I also walk away feeling that I've just been told that those of us who were offended have a problem with hypersensitivity.

While there's a difference between offensive words and a financial crisis, the core principle is the same: apologies that fail to take full responsibility never get anyone off the hook. Far better is the apology that simply says, "I blew it. Here's what happened. Here's where we are. Here's how we plan to fix it."

Once that has taken place, people and congregations are remarkably resilient. There will obviously be naysayers (even Jesus had his share), but most people genuinely want to move on. They simply need to know two things first:

1. Have we gotten the whole truth?
2. Can we trust our leaders to keep telling us the whole truth?

I'm reminded of two churches that I watched deal with severe financial shortfalls. Each handled it in a profoundly different way. One ended up in a death spiral; the other came out stronger than ever.

In one case, the culprit was a pattern of undisciplined spending that had been covered by ever-increasing numerical growth. But after years of flying high, the growth slowed down. Unfortunately, the spending sprees continued. Suddenly, the church wasn't able to pay its bills.

While that was embarrassing, and their actions had been foolhardy, the pastor and board could have saved the day and rallied the troops by putting an instant stop to the expenditures and stepping forward to say, "We made a mistake. We presumed upon growth that didn't happen. We are now seriously in debt. Here's what we are doing to fix it."

Instead, they hid behind doublespeak, excuses, and God-talk. The congregational letters I saw always began with effusive reports of all the great things God was doing in their midst (though everyone could see that things were slowing down, not ramping up). They made vague references to financial shortfalls without details or a game plan, except asking everyone to dig deeper and give more. And they spiritualized everything as an attack from the enemy.

The result was that no one had a clue what was going on. They just knew something was wrong. Worse, each letter seemed to leak a little bit more of the bad news, giving the impression that the pastor and board either didn't know what was going on or were holding back information as long as possible.

In a crisis, people want facts, not fluff. By dancing around the issue and failing to communicate clearly, the pastor further eroded his credibility with each communication. After an initial boost in giving, most people gave less rather than more.

Contrast that with a friend of mine who got himself in a real mess by not paying attention to a construction project that ended up way over budget. When he realized his mistake (and that there was nothing he could do to fix it), he and his team immediately wrote a letter to the entire congregation and addressed the problem in a weekend message.

He told everyone in simple terms what had happened. He apologized and took the blame, even though others he had trusted had let him down by not keeping him abreast of the overruns. He explained what they had already done to rein in expenses. He laid out a plan to get back on track.

No happy talk. No hyperspiritualizing. Just plain English answers that everyone could understand and respond to.

Before writing the letter and addressing the congregation, he called me, concerned that he'd messed up his leadership at the church to such a degree that he'd have to move on.

I told him to expect the opposite. His humility in taking the blame, his courage in telling the truth, and his straightforwardness in laying out a plan would actually endear him to most of the congregation.

I was right. To this day, he looks back on that financial crisis as one of the best things that ever happened to him and the church. It solidified his leadership, it earned him trust and credibility, and it eventually strengthened the church.

Another important thing to ask in a financial crisis is, "Is this really a crisis?" I'm amazed how many churches treat predictable blips as a crisis. The summer slump or the lull before a year-end giving rush is not a crisis. It's an annual event.

Communicating with crisis language is a short-term fix that loses steam every year. It quickly becomes white noise. If and when a real financial crisis hits, people think, "Here we go again. No big deal. It always seems to work out."

That's why I'm always slow to communicate a predictable or temporary slowdown as a crisis. It might put a few extra bucks in the offering plate, but in the long run, it will make communicating in a genuine crisis all the more difficult. I don't want to be the boy who cried, "Wolf!"

So what exactly do we communicate in a financial crisis?

I try to answer for the congregation and staff the same three questions I ask whenever any big problem or crisis crosses my desk:

1. *What happened?* What are the facts? I don't want interpretation, why it happened, or who's at fault; at this stage, I just want the facts.
2. *Why did it happen?* Once again, I'm not asking who's at fault. At this stage, I want to know what were we thinking, what did we miss, and what are the reasons that it happened?
3. *How can we keep it from happening again?* Going forward, what steps will we take or what policies will we follow so that this doesn't happen again?

Releasing Staff

Letting go of a staff member is always a drag. If it's for cause, they still have friends and supporters. If it's part of a financial cutback, there's a sense that this isn't fair, and it isn't. But perhaps the toughest situation is the release of a well-loved but ineffective staff member.

In fact, it's such a drag and so difficult that most churches don't do it. Instead, they let inertia take over, with some complaining behind the scenes. It's frustrating for all involved, but no one knows what to do.

Virtually every time I lead a pastor's roundtable, someone wants to talk about how to deal with a staff member who doesn't cut it, especially the C players who will never do anything bad enough to be fired or good enough to be rehired.

While it's beyond the scope of this chapter to discuss how to deal with an ineffective, lazy, or I'm-in-over-my-head staff member, it's important to note that once the decision has been made to pull the plug and let them go, you're not out of the woods yet.

The communication process can be particularly risky.

I'm not sure it's ever done well, at least not in the sense of everyone being happy with the process and the final outcome. Just as in the case of a moral failure, people will see things differently. But in this case, a lot more people will default to the family paradigm.

But there are some things that we can do to keep this tough and painful situation from unraveling into a full-scale relational disaster. Here are some of the most important ones I've learned over the years.

Accept the Fact That Not Everyone Will Agree

I'm always amazed how much effort and emotional energy is poured into endless conversations trying to make everyone "feel good" about being fired.

It's a waste of time. It will never happen. It reminds me of the gal who breaks off a dating relationship and says, "Let's be friends." It might make her feel good. But everyone knows: friendship is not in the cards.

I'm not saying that we shouldn't be kind, available, or reach out to help. I am saying that lots of people won't agree with your decision. The released staff member will always have friends and supporters who think that you didn't give enough "second chances," others who feel that the church shouldn't be "run like a business," and others who think the person was doing "just fine."

Endless brain debates (the kind we have in our head with someone who isn't there — and we always win) coupled with hours of rehashing the situation with staff members or congregants is like picking at a scab. The wound never heals. It would be nice if we could all hold hands and sing "Kumbaya" at the end of the day. But it's unlikely to happen when you've just told someone, "We don't want you anymore." The pain is simply too great.

Be Generous

When it comes to figuring out a severance package, don't make the mistake of assuming that a generous severance will make a rejected staff member feel better (or even good) about being released. It seldom happens.

But there are still three important reasons to always be as generous as possible.

1. Giving a generous severance package treats others as we'd want to be treated, and I'm pretty sure that Jesus said something about that.
2. It pulls the rug out from under those who want to malign the church and champion the former staff member as a martyr. A generous severance package makes that a hard sell.
3. It acknowledges the church's culpability in the situation. I've always considered it to be ultimately our fault when a staff member didn't work out. Their ineffectiveness is a sign that we failed to train them how to do the job properly or that we hired the wrong person. Either way, it's our fault. A generous severance package is an acknowledgment of our responsibility. It also reminds us to be a lot more careful next time.

Don't Pump Sunshine

One of the most common mistakes pastors and leadership teams make is to extravagantly praise someone they just let go, especially in a churchwide letter or farewell event. While I understand the social pressure to do so, it's a lot like the hollow praise at a scoundrel's funeral. The end result is a loss of credibility.

I learned this the hard way when I wrote a glowing letter praising a staff member I was thrilled to see go. I compounded it by heaping praise on him at his farewell Sunday.

While I was simply trying to be kind, I came off as hypocritical, especially to all those on the inside who knew the whole truth. Some members of the congregation wondered why he was leaving with nowhere to go if he was such a great asset.

I've since learned not to pump sunshine, effusively praising in public someone I criticized in private. Credibility is too important to be squandered in a feel-good meeting. I'd rather have people think I'm a bit of a cold fish than have them think I'm a liar.

That doesn't mean I have to stand on the sidelines at the farewell party with a silly grin on my face. I can be kind. I can honestly find good things to praise. But it's a big mistake to leave people wondering why we let the next best thing to Jesus leave our staff.

In a fallen world, these kinds of tough situations are unavoidable. Even in a great church with a great team, moral failures, financial meltdowns, and staff members who don't make it are part of the landscape. It's not a new phenomenon. The Bible is riddled with similar events.

We can learn a lot by looking at how God responded when things went wrong in Israel and the early church. He didn't cover it up. He told us the truth.

Though painful at times, telling the truth is always the right thing to do. It's also what healthy teams have come to expect and, sadly, what dysfunctional teams will never know.

Final Thoughts

Sticky Teams and the Gates of Hell

AFTER A ROCKY START, I've been incredibly blessed to know the joys, productivity, and impact that flow from a leadership team that has learned how to work and stick together through thick and thin. It's my prayer that you and your church will know it as well.

Not that it's easy to come by. As we've seen in these pages, it takes hard work, some tough calls, and careful attention to details. Unity and health aren't empty platitudes to talk about and hope for. They have to be genuine priorities. They don't just happen because we claim to "love Jesus." They aren't even guaranteed when we genuinely do. Just ask Paul and Barnabas.

I wrote this book to provide some practical guidelines for building and maintaining greater unity and spiritual health within our boards, staffs, and congregations. But one of the best things you can do is to simply discuss together the principles contained in these pages. It will give you a format to expose and talk about the elephants of broken structure, failed tradition, and differing vision, values, or priorities that too often tear teams and churches apart — especially when no one acknowledges their presence or knows how to bring them up.

You'll find a series of follow-up and study questions at the back of the book. Use them to stir the pot and to create a set of shared experiences and a common dictionary. I can't guarantee that it will keep your team from disagreeing. But at least you'll know what you're arguing about.

Finally, be encouraged. Be greatly encouraged. Be filled with joy and optimism. No matter how dysfunctional our churches, boards, or staffs may become, Jesus did promise that he would build his church and that the gates of hell would not hold it back.

Don't miss something important in that promise. The gates of hell aren't an offensive weapon. No one picks up a gate and goes on the attack. Gates are a last line of defense. Jesus wasn't just saying that the church can't be destroyed. He was saying that it won't be held back.

For two thousand years, we've suffered more than our share of failed leadership, astounding cultural blind spots, nasty fights, misplaced priorities, millstone traditions, and lots of sin in the camp. But we've not been able to kill off the church yet. She's still his bride. He's still in love with her, and he's still coming back to take her home.

That alone should give us great confidence. Even when confronted by a pit-bull board member, an Absalom on the staff, or a congregational crazy, the promise still stands. If Satan can't hold off the church, if our forefathers couldn't mess it up beyond repair, we won't kill it either.

So hang tough, my friends.

Remember: in the end, we win.

Discussion Questions

Sticky Teams is designed not only for individual readers but also for leadership teams. Since no two churches are exactly alike, it can be helpful to have your team read the book, digest it, and then discuss which of the principles and concepts best fit your ministry context and which ones don't. Use the following questions as a springboard to get the discussion going. You may also want to add some of your own to make sure that your discussions are tailored to the specific needs of your board, staff, and ministry context.

CHAPTER 1
The Unity Factor: The One Thing That Can't Be Left to Chance

1. What one thing did you agree or disagree with most in this chapter? Why?
2. Osborne contends that unity must be a high priority or it simply won't happen or last very long. Do you agree or disagree? Why?
3. How would you rate our current board's unity in the following areas?

    Doctrinal unity: *high / medium / low*
    Respect and friendship: *high / medium / low*
    Philosophical unity: *high / medium / low*

4. How would you rate our current staff's unity in the following areas?

    Doctrinal unity: *high / medium / low*
    Respect and friendship: *high / medium / low*
    Philosophical unity: *high / medium / low*

5. Complete the following sentences:

    When it comes to unity, our church's greatest strength is ...
    When it comes to unity, our church's greatest weakness is ...

CHAPTER 2

Why Boards Go Bad: Structured for Conflict

1. What did you find most insightful, helpful, or even troubling in this chapter? Why?
2. Do we have any systems, policies, or traditions in our church that unintentionally undercut the unity or effectiveness of our board, staff, or ministry? If so, explain.
3. Osborne lists five roadblocks to unity that his board had to overcome. Which, if any, of these might be a hindrance to our board's effectiveness and unity?

> Meeting in the wrong place
> Ignoring relationships
> Not meeting often enough
> Constant turnover
> Too many board members

CHAPTER 3

Guarding the Gate: No Guts, No Unity

1. What one principle or idea from this chapter did you find most helpful, challenging, or unsettling? Why?
2. On a scale of 1 to 10 (1 = poorly; 10 = carefully), how well does our church guard the gate to lay leadership? How has this impacted the unity and effectiveness of our lay leadership boards in recent years?
3. How much power do "they" have in our board meetings? How much power do "they" have in our staff discussions and programming decisions?
4. Do most of our board members view themselves as representatives or leaders? How does this impact our ministry? Be specific.
5. Historically, what have we looked for most when hiring staff: giftedness, education, character, chemistry, or something else? How has this impacted our staff and ministry?

CHAPTER 4

What Game Are We Playing? How Growth Changes Everything

1. Osborne uses four sports metaphors (track, golf, basketball, and football) to illustrate how the relationships on a leadership team change with growth. Which of these sports best describes the way our *board* currently functions? What game would be most appropriate for our current size, history, and ministry?

2. Which sport best describes the way our *staff* functions? And what game would be most appropriate for the size of our current staff and ministry?

3. Do we have any key players on our board, staff, or in our congregation who are trying to play a different game with a different set of rules? If so, what needs to be done to correct the situation?

4. Which game (pattern of relationships) do you like most and why?

CHAPTER 5

Six Things Every Leadership Team Needs to Know:
Axioms to Lead By

1. Osborne lists six counterintuitive leadership principles. Which ones do you agree with most? Which, if any, do you disagree with?

    Ignore your weaknesses
    Surveys are a waste of time
    Seek permission, not buy-in
    Let squeaky wheels squeak
    Let dying programs die
    Plan in pencil

2. Does our church treat policies as flexible or inflexible? Explain.

3. Does our church treat the annual budget as a guide or a strait-jacket? Explain.

4. Have you ever been on a leadership team where just one contentious or negative person destroyed the effectiveness and morale of the entire team? If so, what happened and what did you learn?

CHAPTER 6

Clarifying the Pastor's Role: Why Leadership Matters

1. What ideas and principles in this chapter did you find most helpful, challenging, or troubling? Why?
2. Osborne offers a list of various roles that a senior pastor can play in a church. Which one do you think is most appropriate for our church? Why?

> Primary leader
> Leader among equals
> Church employee
> Resident mystic (seeking God)
> Chaplain (fulfilling religious functions)

3. Which role do you think most matches the expectations of:

> Our congregation?
> Our board?
> Our staff?
> Our pastor?

CHAPTER 7

Clarifying Board and Staff Roles: Why Teamwork Matters

1. What did you agree with most and least in this chapter?
2. Osborne describes how the role of a board should change as a church grows. Which role best describes how our current board functions? Which one is most appropriate for the current size of our church?

Doing
Approving
Reviewing
Setting direction and boundaries

3. Osborne also describes the way that growth changes the kind of staff members that a church needs. Which roles best describe the way our current staff operates? Which roles are most appropriate to the current size of our church?

Generalist or specialist?
Doing or empowering?
Silo focus or whole church focus?

CHAPTER 8

Making Room at the Top: Why Young Eagles Don't Stay

1. What one insight or principle in this chapter stood out to you most? Why?
2. How would you rate our church's openness to young eagles over the years? Has it changed over time, and if so, how?
3. What constitutes "young" around here? (circle an age bracket)

On the board. *20 – 25 / 25 – 30 / 30 – 35 / 35 – 40 / 40 – 50*
On the staff: *20 – 25 / 25 – 30 / 30 – 35 / 35 – 40 / 40 – 50*

4. When it comes to giving people important roles and influence in our church, what carries the most weight: tenure, gifts, education, or something else? Explain.

CHAPTER 9

Equipped to Lead: Lobbying Isn't Training

1. What one concept or idea in this chapter did you find most helpful or insightful? Why?

2. When our board discusses a new program or idea, do board members usually have time to reflect, or are they asked to make an immediate decision?

3. On a scale of 1 to 10 (1 = poorly; 10 = awesome), how well are we training our board and staff members for their ministry roles? What, if anything, could be done to improve our training and limit our lobbying?

CHAPTER 10

Board Alignment: The Power of an Extra "Shepherds' Meeting"

1. How did the idea of an extra "shepherding meeting" strike you? What did you like most and least about the concept?

2. Do you think our board sets aside adequate time for:

   Team building?
   Training?
   Prayer?

3. Are there any things we could do in the immediate future to improve our:

   Team building?
   Training?
   Prayer?

CHAPTER 11

Staff Alignment: Plumb Lines and Assumptions

1. What three things stood out to you most in this chapter?

2. Does our church have a mission statement? If so, how accurately does it describe the focus and programs of our church?

3. If you had to list three to five of the most important plumb lines or axioms that guide the way our church does ministry, what would they be?

CHAPTER 12

Congregational Alignment: Preempting Conflict

1. What did you resonate with the most and the least in this chapter?
2. How would you rate the underlying level of congregational conflict in our church over the past few years: *high / medium / low*?
3. Osborne offers five tools for preempting congregational conflict. Which, if any, would be good for our church to adopt. Why?

   A clear and simple mission statement
   A frontloaded pastor's class
   Dripping key values into sermons
   Sermon-based small groups
   Short and sweet congregational meetings

CHAPTER 13

Change Diplomacy: Minimizing Conflict and Chaos

1. Do Osborne's four steps of change diplomacy strike you as wise leadership or as manipulation? Explain.
2. Which of the four steps of change diplomacy do we do well? Which ones do we do not so well? Explain.

   Test the waters
   Listen and respond to resisters
   Sell individuals before groups
   Lead boldly

3. When faced with a decision or change that is likely to create some level of significant disappointment or conflict, do we "choose who we lose" or do we try to keep everyone happy? How has that impacted our decisions for good and for bad?

CHAPTER 14

Setting Salaries: Investment or Expense?

1. What did you find most helpful, challenging, or even disconcerting in this chapter? Why?
2. What, if any, factors do we use to determine staff salaries? Are staff members aware of what these factors are?
3. Do we tend to treat staff salaries as an expense or an investment?
4. When it comes to salaries, do we offer our staff members and pastors any opportunity for honest feedback, or is it essentially a take-it-or-leave-it proposition?

CHAPTER 15

Talking about Money: Assumptions, Facts, and a Savings Account

1. This chapter covered some controversial topics. What did you find yourself agreeing with most and least?
2. Do we set our annual budget based primarily on assumptions, or on facts about our income and where it comes from?
3. Do we place any financial or tithing expectation on our staff and board? If not, should we? Why or why not?
4. How does our church view excess income? Do we see unspent savings as hording because of a lack of faith or as a prudent cushion for rainy days? How has this impacted our ministry over the years? How is it impacting it now?

CHAPTER 16

When Things Go Wrong: Telling the Truth When the Truth Is Hard

1. What did you find most helpful in this chapter? What, if anything, did you disagree with the most?

2. Osborne claims that we have to decide ahead of time how we will handle a moral failure or else the competing paradigms of family and justice will likely tear the team apart. Do you agree with him? Why or why not?

3. When it comes time to let a staff member go, do we accept the fact that there is no way to make everyone happy with the decision? If not, how has that impacted the way we deal with difficult staff situations?

Notes

1. Larry Osborne, *The Unity Factor: Developing A Healthy Church Leadership Team* (Vista, Calif.: Owl's Nest, 1989).
2. Larry Osborne, *Sticky Church* (Grand Rapids, Mich: Zondervan, 2008).
3. Eph. 4:3.
4. C. G. Holmans, *The Human Group* (New York: Brace, 1950), 112.
5. See 3 John 9 – 10.
6. See 1 Tim. 3:4 – 5, 12; Titus 1:6.
7. See 1 Tim. 3:1 – 3.
8. See Acts 15:37 – 40.
9. See Matt. 13:57; Mark 6:4; John 4:44.
10. Matt. 20:26 – 28.
11. For a detailed look at how these small groups can slam a church's back door shut, see Osborne, *Sticky Church*.
12. Osborne, *Sticky Church*.
13. This was first noted in the famous job-satisfaction studies of Fredrick Herzberg, *Work and the Nature of Man* (New York: Thomas Y. Cowell, 1966).
14. Prov. 21:20.
15. See James 4:13 – 16.
16. See Acts 5:1 – 11.
17. See James 3:1; 1 Tim. 5:19 – 20; Josh. 7:24 – 25.

STEP OFF THE BEATEN PATH —
Further Readings by Larry Osborne

Take a fresh look at genuine spirituality. Traditional spiritual disciplines and tidy formulas leave some people feeling left out. Osborne cuts through accepted practices and offers a practical paradigm for anyone yearning for a deeper relationship with God.

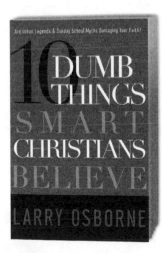

Larry Osborne confronts ten commonly held beliefs that are widely accepted, rarely questioned—and capable of sabotaging genuine faith. Fortunately, behind each misconception hides a powerful truth that has the potential to lead to spiritual freedom, maturity, and dramatic personal change.

MULTNOMAH BOOKS

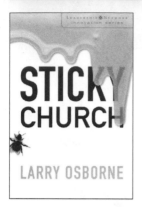